A MANAGER'S GUIDE TO
COMPUTER TIMESHARING

MANAGER'S GUIDE SERIES

A Manager's Guide to Computer Timesharing

TIMOTHY P. HAIDINGER, CPA

Arthur Young & Company
Santa Ana, California

DANA R. RICHARDSON, CPA

Arthur Young & Company
Los Angeles, California

A WILEY-INTERSCIENCE PUBLICATION

John Wiley & Sons
New York · London · Sydney · Toronto

Library of Congress Cataloging in Publication Data:

Haidinger, Timothy P.
  A manager's guide to computer timesharing.

  (Manager's guide series)
  "A Wiley-Interscience publication."
  Bibliography: p.
  1. Electronic data processing—Business.
2. Time-sharing computer systems.   I. Richardson,
Dana R., joint author.   II. Title.

HF5548.2.H32   658'.05'44   74-18413
ISBN 0-471-33925-3

Printed in the United States of America

10 9 8 7 6 5 4 3 2

To

MICHAEL R. MOORE

Series Foreword

In an era in which management science and technology are growing rapidly and at the same time causing great change, one thing remains constant—the manager's need to stay informed. To fulfill his need and to master the new techniques, the manager must understand their workings, grasp their potentials and limitations, and know what questions to ask to ensure that a most efficient job will be done.

This is the premise on which the Manager's Guide Series is based and on which each book is written. The subjects are presented in such a manner as to provide ease of understanding, a grasp of terminology, and a comprehension of potential applications. This approach should enable the manager to understand better the techniques of the management sciences and to apply them to his own needs not as a practitioner but as a mature administrator.

Preface

Earlier volumes in this series have addressed themselves to the need to describe to management the new, more scientific methods of improving business. Operations research, data processing, information systems—each of these subject areas, in turn, has been dealt with by such distinguished authors as Russell L. Ackoff, Roger L. Sisson, and Richard G. Canning.

Following the example of those earlier volumes, this book is a management-oriented explanation of computer timesharing and how it can be used to improve the management of a business enterprise. Perhaps more than any other subject dealt with in this series thus far, computer timesharing is a tool that can be, and is being, used by people at virtually every level of management, in both line and staff functions, for a wide variety of purposes, from record-keeping to financial forecasting to simulation modeling. This book accordingly addresses itself to the needs and interests of many kinds of managers, in different positions and in different industries. While the emphasis inevitably is on those applications of timesharing that tend to be of broad general interest and utility, the book covers a wide range of specialized applications. Its purpose, quite simply, is to be as helpful as possible to as many managers as possible in understanding and using computer timesharing.

We have tried, in effect, to produce the kind of book that would have been valuable to us when we first began to experiment with the use of timesharing in our work as auditors and management consultants some six years ago. Since then we have worked, together and separately, on all sorts of timesharing applications and felt that a cooperative effort would be most fruitful.

Many people have contributed to this book, in many ways. In Arthur Young & Company, the CPA firm with which we are associated, Michael R. Moore, who first encouraged us to get involved in timesharing, deserves special thanks for his continuing counsel and guidance. We are also grateful to David L. James and Robert E. Hanson, the managing partners, respectively, of the firm's Los Angeles and Santa Ana offices, for their enthusiasm and support. And, not least, the authors gratefully acknowledge the many contributions of Albert Newgarden, the firm's director of communications, from the book's inception to its publication, and to his associate May Allstrom for her work in preparing the final manuscript.

We are also grateful to John R. Hillegass, vice president of Datapro Research Corporation, and his colleagues in that organization for permitting us to include substantial portions of their survey report, *All About Remote Computing Services,* in this book. Finally, we acknowledge the assistance of Benedict Kruse in getting it all down on paper.

We enjoyed writing this guide, and hope you enjoy reading it.

Timothy P. Haidinger
Dana R. Richardson

Los Angeles, California
Santa Ana, California
November 1974

Contents

A MANAGER'S GUIDE TO
COMPUTER TIMESHARING

1 The Nature of Computer Timesharing

Computer timesharing, as the name implies, is a technique for sharing access to, and the capabilities of, a computer processor among a number of different users. Depending on the size of the system, individual computers may serve dozens, or even scores, of users concurrently.

The underlying concept of computer timesharing has been likened to the distribution of electric power through large public utilities. Years ago, it is pointed out, it was not uncommon for factories and other enterprises to operate their own power plants. As more powerful generating equipment was developed, however, it became more economical and more reliable for these factories and plants to connect themselves, through power lines, to massive central generators serving many different users in a common geographic area.

Similarly, timesharing users are connected to a central computer facility through communication lines. Recently this analogy has been extended further to cover the increasingly frequent phenomenon of power brownouts. Thus when a computer timesharing facility becomes overloaded through a failure in design or planning, it is said that the service, like the output of a power generator, becomes "degraded."

Although this analogy is useful and basically valid, there is an important difference between an electric utility and a timesharing system—one that is particularly significant to the manager. A power generator can distribute its output to thousands of users simultaneously, sharing its end products indiscriminately. With a timeshared computer, however, utilization is both total and staggered—that is, in the majority of cases, each sequence of operations performed by a particular computer at a particular time is devoted to handling a single user problem. The "sharing" takes place by rotating the utilization of infinitesimal time segments. Because computers can execute operational commands in split millionths of a second, it is possible for a number of user jobs to be processed concurrently, with the computer swapping small time segments between literally dozens of separate tasks.

CHARACTERISTICS OF A TIMESHARING SYSTEM

Computer timesharing is a broad field that presents many different faces to different people. Accordingly, there are a number of different ways of defining or describing timesharing systems, each more or less appropriate according to the particular system and/or the particular user needs in question. From a broad management point of view, however, a computer timesharing system can be defined in terms of four basic characteristics:

1. **Serves multiple users concurrently.** Each user is served as though the computer were his own. This is an important consideration to management, because the same capabilities that enable a timeshared computer system to serve multiple users individually also play a critical part in providing the high degree of control and reliability that management needs and expects from a computer system. The ability to serve multiple users concurrently also holds the key to the economics of timesharing: sharing of use implies—and provides a logical basis for—sharing of costs.

2. **Serves remote users through on-line access.** Remote access to the timeshared computer is provided through simple, low-cost terminal devices that lack both the sophistication and the complexity of the input consoles common to most computer installations. The typical timesharing terminal is not much more complex than an ordinary typewriter; there are no

batteries of status lights, control dials, or other technical displays. As the term "on-line" implies, these terminals have direct access, on demand, to the computer system; no intermediate processing or other intervention is necessary between the terminal user and the central computer. Such on-line access is a characteristic of all timesharing operations, regardless of whether entries are made one character at a time or large volumes of data are transmitted for processing in "batches" from remote locations.

3. **Provides service on a real-time basis.** The term "real-time" implies that computer processing is performed and results delivered within the actual time requirements of individual user jobs—that is, the processing needed to complete task A is performed before task B is initiated, the processing needed to complete task B before task C, and so on. Thus a "real-time" reaction for a computer monitoring an industrial process might be a fraction of a second. A customer at a teller's window in a bank, on the other hand, might find real-time service adequate if the computer responded in three to five seconds. And a financial manager wishing a report on the status of outstanding accounts receivable might be satisfied if he receives the results the following morning. In each of these cases, the computer functions according to individual user commands; data are accepted when the user submits them; and responses are provided within the time frame and format requested by the user. This characteristic represents a major difference between timesharing and conventional batch processing.

For example, the manager who delivers a deck of punched cards to his company's data-processing department or to a service bureau in the evening for processing of reports to be delivered the next morning will experience no interim results of computer processing. His first feedback will occur when he receives the reports, whether they are acceptable or not. By contrast, the same data entered through a timesharing terminal will be validated and determined to be acceptable *at the time of input*. Should there be any errors or exception conditions, the computer will advise the user immediately, so that any necessary corrections or adjustments can be made before the data are processed. Thus there is a greater probability that the results received the next morning will be valid and usable.

4. **Permits the user to impact the data content of the system.** This characteristic serves to distinguish between true timesharing systems, which process user data and deliver results according to the user's instructions, and other types of remote-access on-line computer systems which permit only inquiries from files that the user cannot impact. An example of a non-impact on-line inquiry system is the popular stock quotation service used by most securities dealers: the individual broker has access only to data generated by someone else, and thus has no impact on the data content of the system. In a timesharing system, by contrast, the user constantly introduces new data that serve as a basis for, and affect the results of, the computer's processing. For example, when an agent at an airline reservations desk performs an inquiry function to determine the availability of seats on a given flight, he is not impacting the data content of the system, but when he sells a ticket, he changes the content of the files that control the availability of seats.

HOW THE SYSTEM FUNCTIONS

A timesharing system functions as a closed-loop communication network under the control of the user. The user generates both data and instructions to the timesharing system at his terminal device. The terminal itself is selected for familiarity and compatibility with the user's environment and special needs. Thus some terminals are based on simple ten-key adding machines. Others resemble ordinary ball-type typewriters or conventional teletypewriters. Still others use television-like cathode-ray tubes to display data on screens.

At the user's command, data are transmitted from the terminal to the computer via communication lines. Most commonly, these are telephone lines—either special leased lines or part of the ordinary dial network.

The central computer installation itself includes a communication controller, a central processor, and large banks of peripheral devices that store and handle data. In response to user commands, the computer selects appropriate programs for processing and activates any data files required to perform the assigned task.

The computer controls the generation of its end products and the delivery of results to the user—according to the user's instructions in those cases where responses are not immediate. In some situations, the computer actually interacts with the timesharing user in what is known as "conversational mode." Within the limits imposed by specific data-processing tasks to be done and programs used, the computer carries on a dialogue with the user through printed or displayed messages originated by the computer and corresponding responses entered into the terminal keyboard by the user.

An example of a short transaction in conversational mode is shown in Figure 1.1. This brief segment is from a timesharing program designed to deliver interest data to bank loan officers for use in complying with the truth-in-lending laws. The particular conversation shown in Figure 1.1 deals with add-on interest for an automobile loan. The computer starts the conversation by asking for the add-on interest rate. When this has been provided by the user, the computer asks for the number of months of the loan's duration. When the user responds that the loan will be for 36 months, the computer generates the needed answer immediately.

It is obvious from this example that it does not take a trained programmer or computer operator to use a timesharing system. When appropriate, the system may in fact be set up with "lead-through" capabilities, so that the computer actually tells the operator what entries to make to execute a program.

WHAT IS THE ADD-ON INTEREST RATE?   .07

WHAT IS THE TERM OF THE NOTE IN MONTHS?   36

THE EFFECTIVE INTEREST RATE IS   .1282

Figure 1.1 Transaction in conversational mode.

The power that a computer timesharing system can deliver is well illustrated by one of the earliest business applications of timesharing—airline reservation systems. In such systems, a single computer, centrally located, keeps track of the reservation status of several hundred daily flights for more than a month into the future. Records of passengers' names, telephone numbers, travel agent identifications, seat assignments, special meal requirements, and other service factors run literally into billions of characters of data—all of which are available for inquiry from thousands of stations, throughout the United States, in a maximum of two to three seconds.

Timesharing systems may be established on either a utility or a proprietary basis. *Utility-type timesharing systems* offer services to subscribers on a fee basis. In such systems, the cost structure is generally based on actual utilization of services—number of terminals connected to the system and/or actual processor time used by the customer, plus a small fee for the storage of data on peripheral files of the computer system. *Proprietary, or "in-house," timesharing systems* are operated by a single company or a group of companies (sometimes related, sometimes unrelated except through their joint ownership of the timesharing system) to provide specific services to preidentified users. Thus a state or regional hospital association might establish a proprietary timesharing system for the use of member hospitals.

The basic characteristics of timesharing, described earlier, apply to both utility and proprietary systems. However, considerations affecting the management, use, and economics of the two types of systems are quite different. This book is concerned primarily with the use of utility-type timesharing systems by business managers. It does not deal with the substantial planning and development effort involved in establishing a proprietary system, nor with the economics of such systems.

The actual functioning of a utility-type timesharing service is discussed in greater detail in Chapter 2.

THE VALUE OF TIMESHARING TO MANAGEMENT

The benefits that management can derive from timesharing vary according to both size of the company and individual management requirements.

The manager of a small enterprise—particularly a company involved in manufacturing or distribution—is likely to view timesharing promiarily as a means of applying computer capabilities to his business needs without incurring the extensive investment in equipment and staff that have deterred him from developing his own computer processing facility in the past. With timesharing, this manager acquires a known, proven product for an established price. Even if the service rendered is not exactly what he wants, or is not tailored specifically to his company's needs, the tradeoffs in economy and immediate availability are likely to weigh heavily in his judgment. In addition, it is likely to occur to this manager that, with timesharing, he is not locked into a long-term commitment, as he would be if he bought or leased equipment and hired skilled employees. Even if the results delivered by a timeshared computer should fall short of management expectations, the timesharing approach provides an always-accessible exit.

For a manager in a larger company with existing computer operations of its own, the use of timesharing affords an opportunity both for handling overflow processing needs and for developing special-purpose management tools. The data-processing department in a large company may find certain specific programs or services offered by a timesharing utility economically attractive as a basis for expanding its own services, for introducing new services on a startup basis, or for shifting workloads temporarily or seasonally. In other situations, particularly where the data-processing department operates on a batch basis only, the immediate access and control that timesharing affords may be attractive for special, mathematically oriented management functions.

The various kinds and qualities of service available through timesharing utilities are discussed at greater length in Chapter 3.

AN HISTORICAL PERSPECTIVE

The development of timesharing has been quite rapid—and, as typically happens under such circumstances, the growth of the industry has been characterized both by solid accomplishments and by inability to live up to some of the glowing predictions and promises of early enthusiasts. As with many other developments that have emerged from a theoretical scientific environment, imagination has often outdistanced accomplishment. In the early 1960s, the potential of timesharing was seen as approaching infinity. By the early seventies, the focus had shifted from such early blue-sky visions to a reality that, while short of infinity, represented a significant advancement nonetheless.

At its inception, timesharing was viewed essentially as a means of using large-scale computers more efficiently. In running a single problem, technicians pointed out, a high-capacity processor idled—frequently and repeatedly—for periods of a tenth of a second or more for file references and other "housekeeping" chores. If the large-scale computer could serve multiple users, it was reasoned, it might, through continuing productivity, be able to pay its way—a possibility that was then in serious doubt in some quarters.

One of the first public expressions of this viewpoint came from Christopher Strachey, a British mathematician. In a paper on timesharing concepts delivered at an international conference on information processing sponsored by UNESCO in 1959, Dr. Strachey said in part:

Keeping a steady flow of problems to the machine is obviously going to present very great difficulties, and I do not think it will be possible not to lose a few seconds between each problem. It seems worthwhile considering timesharing between operators, so that if one operator is idling another may be using the machine.

The first implementation of this concept took place in 1961, with the completion of design and initial demonstration of a scientifically oriented timesharing system at the Massachusetts Institute of Technology. This initial facility was known as Project MAC (represented at various times as an acronym either for

Machine-Aided Cognition or for Multiple-Access Computer). Operational use of Project MAC by the scientific community at MIT began in 1963. The prime innovators of this milestone system were Professors R. M. Fano and F. J. Corbato.

The remarkable enthusiasm generated by this initial demonstration of timesharing is evidenced by the fact that a number of other systems were off and running within a year. The first commercial organization to implement a timesharing system was Bolt Beranek and Newman, Inc., headquartered in Cambridge, Massachusetts. This organization built a system that served as a basis for later, expanded efforts in medical diagnostics through the use of computers.

In 1964, the System Development Corporation of Santa Monica, California, introduced both a timesharing system and a software language designed specifically for direct interaction with computers by relatively untrained users. This work, performed under the direction of Jules Schwartz, produced the widely used language known as JOVIAL (Jules' Own Version of an Interactive Algorithmic Language).

Another significant milestone in user techniques came at Dartmouth College. Under Dr. Thomas Kurtz and Professor John Kemeny, data-processing and research personnel developed the BASIC (Beginner's All-purpose Symbolic Instruction Code) language, which has since become the most widely used general-purpose programming language in timesharing systems.

Significantly, the development of business applications for timesharing paralleled the scientific mainstream—though it was years before the business and scientific applications were considered elements of a single entity. In part, this was because early developments in the business world concentrated on special-purpose systems. The pioneering business use of timesharing techniques was the SABRE reservations system developed for American Airlines. The commitment for the development of this system was initiated in 1959, and the system was operational in the same time frame as the university systems cited above.

By 1964, the Dime Savings Bank of Brooklyn had implemented a multibranch system for savings accounting. Shortly thereafter, the National Cash Register Company, which had provided the equipment for Dime, began offering utility-type timesharing services for savings accounting to savings banks and savings and loan associations.

In retrospect, it can be said that scientific practitioners gave timesharing its basic dimensions while businessmen provided the pragmatism necessary for it to fulfill its potential. By the late 1960s, business and scientific applications were viewed as part of a single entity. Business utilization for both routine day-to-day processing applications and scientific management techniques has served to provide the basis for the emergence of timesharing as a viable commercial enterprise.

In its long developmental journey through the sixties, timesharing left many casualties along the wayside—punctured investment pipedreams. Inevitably, there has been some bitterness. Realistically, however, timesharing today must be regarded as a here-and-now reality, and an important tool of modern management. That is the premise of this book, and its purpose is to help managers use this new tool to their own and their companies' advantage.

2 Basic Elements of a Timesharing System

The distinctive characteristics of computer timesharing, on a utility-type service basis, can perhaps best be described by comparing the way a simple data-processing job would be handled by an ordinary batch computer system with the way the same job would be handled by a timesharing system.

BATCH COMPUTER SYSTEMS

By far the greatest volume of business data processing today is still handled by batch computer systems—so called because the documents or transactions to be processed are grouped and entered into the computer in "batches," thus achieving a relatively high degree of control at a relatively low cost. In effect, a batch computer system is a production shop much like a factory that fabricates and assembles products. The batch of documents or transactions corresponds roughly to a lot of parts or components processed through the factory: The work moves from one station to another; at each station, the operator does a certain job for which his equipment is specifically set up; and then the work moves on to the next station.

Extending this analogy to a common business information-handling situation, a wholesale company typically processes and assembles incoming orders in batches. Some orders are brought or mailed in from the field by salesmen; others are written by telephone order-takers. In either case, it is typical to group anywhere from 50 to 150 incoming orders for processing. These are edited for accuracy and acceptability of customer and item designations. Control totals are then developed for each batch of orders. These totals are generally entered on batch control tickets. Controls frequently used for order entry are total dollar value of the batch, number of orders in the batch, and number of line items of merchandise covered. The batches of documents are then carried physically from the order or sales department to the data-processing department.

Within a well-run data-processing shop, incoming batches of work are received by a data control section or group. Each job is logged in so that it can be accounted for through delivery. Batches of documents are routed first from the control group to a data conversion section which, through some type of key-entry devices, captures data on the order forms in machine-readable media—punched cards, magnetic tape, or magnetic disk. In most cases, some form of verification or validation takes place in the data conversion section. This can be done by repeating the key entries, by creating balance documents that will be validated by the computer before processing takes place, or by a combination of both.

For computer processing it is frequently necessary to accumulate a number of batches of documents to build up enough volume to justify setup requirements. At a minimum, the necessary order or invoice forms must be mounted on a computer printer before processing takes place. At the time the job is run, the order-invoice program either takes over the entire computer system or, with a multiprogramming computer, occupies an entire processing partition.

Each batch of data is then run in its entirety Should there be invalid or unacceptable transactions, they are processed as exceptions and must be reentered in a later batch or processed manually as exceptions. Should a batch be out of balance, human intervention is necessary. Corrections or adjustments must be made before the processing can go forward.

Each batch of orders or invoices processed by the computer is then logged by the data control group and delivered physically to the department that will use the documents next.

THE TIMESHARING APPROACH

In a timesharing system, each unit of data is processed as it is generated. Processing takes place through direct interaction between the person originating the data—the timesharing user—and the computer system.

Instead of requiring whole batches of documents for economic handling, the timesharing computer will accept and process a very small number of data per transaction. Thus the entire data entry process can be completed at the point at which a transaction actually takes place. In an order department, for example, telephone order personnel would work directly on data terminals linked to the timeshared computer through communication lines. Interaction takes place through the item-by-item editing and validation of data by the computer or through controls within the terminal as the operator enters the data.

In initiating a customer order, the terminal operator, either taking data on the phone or working from an abbreviated order form generated by a salesman, enters only the customer number—or an identification code if the file number is unavailable. With just this minimal information entered, the operator depresses a key, which triggers transmission of the data to the computer. If a customer number has been entered, the computer looks up the account in its files and sends back a message to the terminal, which causes customer identification (including shipping instructions and credit limits, as appropriate) to be typed out on a form or displayed on a screen. If a code derived from the customer's name and address has been entered, the computer will look up the account through cross-reference, then enter the number as well as descriptive information.

For each item ordered, the terminal operator then enters the part number and the quantity desired. The computer will use this information to refer to its files for product description, warehouse location, price, discount structures, quantity on hand, the possible need for reordering, and other information. In the pages that follow, the processing of this simple transaction will be traced in greater detail—in terms of both timesharing system elements and data content.

THE USER'S TERMINAL

The modern timesharing user has literally hundreds of terminal devices to choose from, according to his functional requirements and economic considerations. These range from simple adding machines adapted for direct computer input, through typewriter and teletypewriter devices, to cathode-ray-tube terminals with video screens, "intelligent" terminals with electronic processing capabilities of their own, and terminal devices that are actually small computers themselves.

At the lower end of the computer terminal family—in terms of both cost and sophistication—is the simple numeric device. At the least-cost level, touch-tone telephones are used as computer entry terminals. Ten-key and full-keyboard adding machines have also been adapted as computer terminals. A typical numeric-only terminal is shown in Figure 2.1.

At the next level of sophistication and expense, alphabetic entry and printout capabilities are added. The least costly terminal device of this type is the teletypewriter. Specifically, the Teletype Model ASR 33 (**A**utomatic **S**end-**R**eceive) is probably the most widely used timesharing or data entry terminal in the world. The teletypewriter has the advantage of being both universal and relatively inexpensive. Disadvantages are comparatively slow speed, limited capacity in terms of type fonts and line widths, and comparatively heavy weight. A typical teletypewriter terminal is shown in Figure 2.2.

A somewhat greater degree of sophistication for relatively little additional cost can be attained through typewriter-type terminals using ball-mechanism printing devices (Figure 2.3). The most

Figure 2.1 Numeric-only terminal.

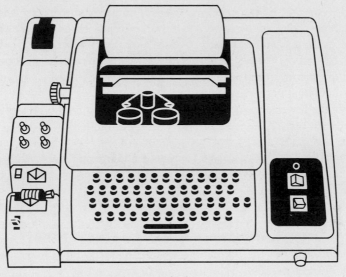

Figure 2.2   Teletypewriter terminal.

popular terminal of this type is the IBM 2741. This device is approximately 50 percent faster than the teletypewriter, and also offers interchangeable type fonts and wider page formats. Devices of this type are also more compatible with the feeding and print-ing out of continuous business forms. (Thus invoice forms pre-pared on a terminal of this type can be easily kept in alignment under control of the computer program.) Some devices using ball-type printers can be regarded as semiportable. Terminals of this type can be used as normal office typewriters when they are not linked to the computer.

Another, quite popular, type of user terminal is compatible with both the teletypewriter and the ball typewriter. This is the lightweight, highly flexible heat-transfer typewriter. These devices make their imprint through the proximity of a matrix of heated wires to sensitive paper. Heat-transfer devices are potentially faster than either of the two other typewriter-oriented terminals; they can, in fact, be twice as fast as a ball-type unit. However, most such devices are designed for variable-speed operation, so

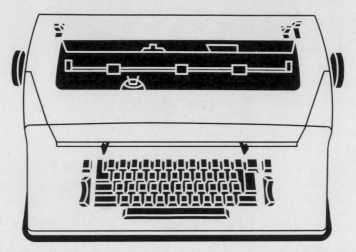

Figure 2.3   Typewriter-type terminal with ball-mechanism printing device.

that they are fully compatible with either of the other typewriter-type terminals.

Heat-transfer terminals represent a next step up in cost and versatility. As a rule of thumb, they are about 50 percent more costly than teletypewriters. (On a lease basis, however, all three units are comparable in cost, largely because of compensating differences in maintenance requirements.) A minor, but not insignificant, consideration relating to the use of heat-transfer terminals is that special treated paper is required. Paper costs are thus somewhat higher—but the availability of treated paper can be a more important consideration than cost. The legibility and reproduction quality of documents printed by heat-transfer devices are not as good as those of documents produced by impact-type printers. On the other hand, the elimination of impact makes for a far quieter terminal device. An example of a heat-transfer terminal is shown in Figure 2.4.

A comparatively large jump in both cost and capabilities is experienced in moving from imprint-type terminals such as those described above to display-type units—specifically, those that display data on cathode-ray-tube (CRT) screens. These units use a video screen to display data that are either generated by the computer or entered into a keyboard by the operator. Most CRT terminals have display-regenerating capabilities that make it possible to enter comparatively large volumes of data and store them on the screen while they are being edited and revised as necessary. Then, on a simple command from the user, all of the data on the screen can be transmitted to the computer in a single transaction. As compared with a teletypewriter, for example, a typical CRT terminal can transmit up to 25 times as much data in a single transaction—at up to 48 times the speed. However, a typical CRT terminal costs more than twice as much as a teletypewriter or a ball-type printer.

A disadvantage of CRT terminals that may rule them out for a particular user application is that they provide no printed record of entries or transactions—unless a separate printing device is incorporated into the terminal configuration at additional cost. Again, it should be noted that CRT terminals generate almost no noise. Because of their ability to display substantial quantities of data rapidly and quietly, CRT terminals are very popular as executive information devices. A typical CRT terminal is shown in Figure 2.5.

For still greater sophistication, many timesharing users have installed "intelligent" terminals or terminal systems built around

Figure 2.4   Heat-transfer terminal.

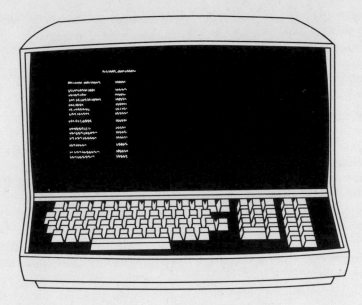

Figure 2.5   Cathode-ray-tube (CRT) terminal.

minicomputers. Intelligent terminals, in general, are those that use electronic memories to control sequences of data entry in comparatively sophisticated applications or in situations where multiple applications are being processed from one location. Intelligent terminals frequently have some calculating capacity, but they fall far short of true computer capabilities.

Many user terminals do, however, actually incorporate small computers for local processing of transactions. These devices are used in situations where it is possible to process transactions remotely, then transmit data in batches to a central timesharing computer for file updating.

One example of such a minicomputer terminal is the device used to collect demand deposit transaction data from independent banks or branches. This device, controlled by a minicomputer, uses a document sorter that reads magnetic characters on checks or deposit slips. Data are collected on magnetic tape for transmission to a central computer, which updates account files. While the central computer is processing the files, the sorter on the terminal, under minicomputer control, sequences the checks at the bank. This type of terminal frequently has a high-speed printer for preparing statements used in bank operations.

CRITERIA FOR SELECTING A TERMINAL

Application requirements should be the primary consideration in the selection of terminals for timesharing utilization. Specifically, the value of the timesharing application to the user organization should be the most important factor in justifying capacities, characteristics, and expenditures for terminal equipment. Application requirements that may affect terminal selection decisions include speed, memory and edit capabilities, off-line storage, hard-copy requirements, line width, type fonts, portability, and programmability.

Speed

The operating speed of a terminal can affect both the productivity and the responsiveness of a timesharing system. If the volume of data printed is an important consideration, for example, the terminal's printing speed can be a critical selection factor.

Speed of operation can also affect the overall cost of timesharing utlization. In many systems, part of the fee charged by a timesharing utility reflects the amount of time a terminal is connected to the system. A faster terminal could well pay for itself by reducing this "connect" time.

Memory and Edit Capabilities

The capacity of a terminal to store data prior to their transmission to the timesharing system can have a significant impact on accuracy and quality. If, for example, an operator at the order desk enters an item number and quantity, it can be valuable to delay transmission of these data to the computer until the operator can read the numbers back to the caller on the telephone or compare them against the source document from which he or she is typing.

Editing capability comes into play at two levels. The first is at the terminal itself: if the operator notices an entry error, it can be valuable to have the ability to make a correction at the terminal, before the transaction is entered into the computer.

Another aspect of editing capability involves interacting with the central computer to edit and correct data before they are actually processed. Assume, for example, that the operator transmits an invalid item number that corresponds with the entry on his source document. The computer would send back a signal indicating that this is not a valid product number. The operator, depending on the characteristics of the individual terminal, may be able to correct the entry if he has access to accurate data or, failing this, can instruct the computer to cancel the item prior to processing.

Some terminals, particularly CRT units, have enough memory capacity that the entire transaction can be displayed and the operator can correct only those data elements that are in error. Considerable savings can be realized by eliminating the need for complete reentry of entire transactions.

Off-Line Storage

In high-volume applications particularly, it may be desirable to automate the transmission and receipt of data from computers. To accomplish this, data entered at a terminal are recorded on a storage medium such as punched tape, magnetic tape, cassettes, and disks. Data are accumulated on these media for transmission at speeds which are, in some cases, hundreds of times faster than manual key-stroking. This can result in substantial economies in transmission and processing time. In some situations, this approach might also make it possible to use computers at other than peak hours, further reducing fees.

When data are accumulated on storage media for subsequent entry in bulk, the process is frequently referred to as "remote batch processing." This timesharing technique will be discussed further in a later chapter.

The availability of off-line storage can also make it possible to apply high-speed printing devices at the user location. One typical technique calls for receiving processed data from the computer on magnetic tape, then using this tape on off-line printers which typically have speeds of 300 to 500 lines per minute.

Off-line storage can also be important in protecting data files against accidental loss or destruction. For example, data recorded on magnetic tape for transmission to a computer can be stored in this format until there is assurance that all transactions have been properly received and processed. Similarly, processed data can be received and recorded on magnetic tape for storage at the user site as a protection against loss or malfunction at the central computer site.

Hard-Copy Requirements

If the user needs a printed record of timesharing transactions, this will be an important consideration in his choice of computer terminals or terminal configurations. As noted earlier, a straight-forward CRT terminal does not create a printed record of trans-actions. Thus if transaction records are needed for reference or control, special provision must be made for creating such records if a CRT terminal is to be used.

Line Width

Teletypewriter terminals are limited to 72 character positions per line. Ball-type and line-printer terminals are available in 132-character widths. Depending on the format and content of re-quired documents, line width can obviously be a significant factor affecting the selection of terminals.

Type Fonts

Occasionally, as in the case of credit letter follow-up on accounts receivable files, it is desirable to produce documents that look as though they were individually typed. This requires the availability of both upper- and lowercase type fonts. Some terminals—par-ticularly teletypewriters and heat-transfer units—do not have this capability. If such applications are important, the user will have to select either a ball-type terminal or a configuration with an off-line printer with upper- and lowercase capabilities.

Portability

In some applications it may be desirable to enter data from terminals that can be moved with the user. Some companies, for example, have systems in which salesmen enter their orders on-line from customer offices, from hotel rooms, or from their homes. In other instances, managers carry terminals with them to perform data analyses as part of meetings. And, sometimes, timesharing services are made available to the manager who simply likes to take his work home evenings or weekends. In all of these situations, the weight and bulk of the terminals are, obviously, important considerations.

Programmability

Where data entries will be made on terminals by either low-level employees or persons who use the computer system infrequently, it may be valuable to secure terminals with "lead-through" capabilities. Such units can store programs either in off-line media or in electronic memories for the programming of input transaction formats. In effect, these programs tell the operator what data should be entered at each step in a fixed program. This approach has proved valuable in such applications as retail and bank transactions.

COMMUNICATION LINKS

The transmission and reception of data to and from a computer require a highly reliable electronic conversion process in most instances. In general, data are generated and processed by both terminals and computers in coded formats utilizing patterns of binary bits. Transmission of data over communication lines requires a conversion of data from an electromechanical or magnetic storage format to electrical communication signals. These signals represent tones that are audible only when used to drive a suitable speaker-like or diaphragm device such as a telephone receiver.

On receipt, the signals or tones are reconverted to equivalent electrical energy to rerecord the data mechanically or magnetically.

The devices that perform this conversion process at both the sending and receiving ends of a communication line are known as either *modems* or *Data Sets*. (The word "modem" is an acronym for the function "*mo*dulate-*dem*odulate." Modulation is the conversion of impulses to tones; demodulation is the reverse.) Data Sets are a specific type of modem installed by Bell System companies. The modem, in effect, is the telephone station through which a terminal talks to the timesharing computer. In most cases, Data Sets include telephone instruments and dials.

The actual connection of terminals to modems is accomplished in either of two ways:

1. **The terminal can be "hard-wired" to the modem.** This indicates that the wiring of the terminal is connected directly into the transmitter/receiver unit.
2. **The modem can incorporate an audio coupler.** With this approach, the connection is established between the terminal location and the computer on an ordinary voice-grade dial telephone. The telephone handset is inserted into the audio coupler of the modem, which then generates or reads tones into or from the telephone instrument.

The hard-wire installation is more reliable, of higher quality, and of greater permanence. However, this approach requires professional installation, represents a longer-term commitment, and is less flexible.

By comparison, audio coupling is more subject to line interference but far more flexible. With this technique, timesharing service can be established or discontinued at any point where the user has a telephone instrument.

Timesharing transmissions can be carried over many different kinds of communication lines. In general, line costs are directly related to the transmission capacity and length of a given line.

The least expensive, lowest-capacity transmission line is known as a *half-duplex* circuit. This is simply a circuit with two wires— one signal line and a return, or ground—between two points. With a half-duplex or two-wire circuit, data can be transmitted in only one direction at a time. Thus a terminal cannot be receiving data from the computer while the operator is sending data. This type of communication link has been used primarily for telegraphic service.

The next step up is to use a four-wire, or *full-duplex,* circuit. This is the type of connection normally established for telephone conversations. Most timesharing services today use full-duplex circuits. These can be acquired either through dial service or on a leased-line basis. (With leased-line service, a full-duplex line is rented on a regular basis from telephone common carriers.) In general, a full-duplex line has the capacity to transmit or receive at a rate of up to 2400 baud, or bits of data per second. This is equivalent to approximately 240 characters per second.

Consideration of this line capacity gives further dimension to earlier discussions of terminal speed and automated transmission from off-line storage media. Recorded data can be transmitted at speeds of up to 240 characters per second. However, even under automatic operation, printing terminals are limited to 30 characters per second—and a typist entering data directly from a keyboard is effectively limited to seven or eight characters per second.

Where data transmission requirements are greater, additional lines can be added. In general, communication lines with capacities greater than full-duplex are known as *broadband* service. Transmission capabilities are directly proportional to the lines available. Thus four lines would make a transmission rate of 4800 baud available, eight lines would carry 9600 baud, and so on. Services regularly available from telephone carriers extend to 32 lines. However, users of timesharing utility services will rarely require or encounter services involving more than full-duplex lines.

In some cases, however, timesharing utilities do use a technique known as *multiplexing* to concentrate transmission from a number of users over the same telephone lines. Multiplexors are satellite communication processors. (Minicomputers are often used for multiplexing.) A large number of timesharing users, sometimes as many as 132, can be linked to a single multiplexing

point. Their transmissions are then carried from the multiplexor
to the central computer over either full-duplex or broadband
lines. Typically, a multiplexor will be set up in a city remote from
the central computer. For example, many timesharing companies
operate computers in New York. These organizations then establish multiplexing points in major cities such as Chicago and Los
Angeles, where users can link into the national timesharing network through local telephone calls.

THE TIMESHARING CENTER

The timesharing service center is a computer facility with a configuration established especially for processing communication
traffic, processing large volumes of data, and storing large files.
A timesharing installation has three major elements: a communication processor, the central processor, and peripheral equipment.

Communication Processor

A communication processor is actually a separate computer set
up and programmed especially to handle communications with
users. In some installations, the communication processor also
handles "housekeeping" functions such as file referencing and
printing.

In general, the communication processor polls user "portals"
into the timesharing system. The computer actually establishes a
connection, in rotation, with each data entry point in the system.
When the computer senses that there is a message to be transmitted, it accepts the data, assembles the message within its own
memory, validates the format of the message, and then establishes
a signal, or flag, to indicate to the main computer that there is a
message to be processed.

In many systems the communication processor will acknowledge
receipt of data to the transmitting terminal. In some systems this
is done through a technique known as "echoing." Under this
approach, the communication computer actually repeats the message to the terminal to validate the transaction.

The communication processor also serves as a transmitter of data from the computer center back to the terminals.

The Central Processor

The central processing unit of a timesharing system is a medium- or large-scale computer designed or specially equipped for rapid interruption and processing of data in short spurts. The central processor must have both the necessary software and the capacity to keep track of a large number of programs which may be in active use at any given time. It must also have the capacity to establish and maintain tables to control the locations of a large number of programs and files in memory and storage.

Depending on the nature of the timesharing equipment and its associated software or control programs, the central processor may also perform other, nontimesharing, activities (e.g., local batch processing) at the same time.

For example, when a transaction for an invoicing operation is received at the central processor, the computer senses, from identifiers built into the terminal, which user is involved. The computer calls that user's program into its main memory from peripheral storage. In initiating the transaction, the computer determines that a file reference is necessary to call up the record for the product being ordered. The computer then determines that this file reference will involve more idle time than it can afford for waiting. Accordingly, it picks up the next transaction from the same user or goes to a program of an entirely different user. The program of the second user can then be processed until the computer reaches a new file reference point. At this juncture, if the record for the invoicing program is ready, it is processed.

As the central processor switches back and forth between programs and files, it updates its own tables to indicate the status of all processing. At the same time, the computer generates a continuing stream of records which serve as the basis for user billing.

Peripherals

Peripheral equipment for timesharing systems derives its importance from the level of support provided for users. On this basis, the most important peripherals associated with a timesharing installation are massive random-access storage units. The great bulk of timesharing files are stored on disk devices. However, some timesharing systems do use lower-cost magnetic-card peripherals such as IBM Data Cells or NCR CRAM files.

Disk files are of two types—movable read/write head units (with interchangeable packs of disks) and fixed-head units. In a movable-head disk file, the read/write device actually moves back and forth above the surface of the disk to select the proper recording track. On a fixed-head unit, there is a permanent read/write head over each recording track. With a fixed head, any item of data can be read or recorded in one rotation of the disk. By contrast, considerably larger fractions of a second are necessary for a movable head to position itself over the proper track, and then to wait for disk rotation to the needed point.

As a reference or file maintenance device, then, the fixed-disk unit is obviously more efficient. However, a comparison of the two types of file devices would involve a discussion of cost and performance tradeoffs which is beyond the scope and purpose of this book.

Random-access files are also stored on magnetic drums. On drum units, data are stored magnetically on the exterior surfaces of a rotating cylinder. A fixed head is mounted above each recording track. Drum and fixed-disk files are similar in performance and cost.

Most timesharing systems include *tape drives* among their peripherals. Magnetic tape is used, to a large extent, for the logging of transactions entered into and processed by a timesharing computer. Tape files serve, among other purposes, as backup for the random-access files. Should a random-access file be destroyed accidentally, backup files and tape can be used to reconstruct records on a current basis. The logs on magnetic tapes are also used by computer utilities to bill their customers. Tape drives can also be used for backup storage and loading of user programs.

A *high-speed printing* capability is also a peripheral necessity for a timesharing installation. Such printers are frequently used to draw off massive data reports which would be too cumbersome to produce through communication line transmission. These reports can then be delivered to users by mail or messenger. A time-sharing utility also needs a high-speed printing capability to generate its own operating reports, user bills, and so on.

For entry of massive user file conversions or programs too large for efficient on-line preparation, most timesharing installations have a *punched-card reader*. Generally, there are also one or more *terminals* through which operators communicate with the computer.

All told, a timesharing center is a collection of highly self-sufficient, interrelated equipment in a configuration designed for continuous, reliable service. The various services provided by such a facility, and what they mean to users, are discussed in the following chapter.

3 Using a Timesharing Utility Service

In user terms, timesharing utility services can be said to fall into two basic categories:

1. **Utility services that are fully preprogrammed.** The user takes advantage of existing "packages." He saves programming and startup costs. But he loses flexibility in being able to adapt programs to his specific needs. Applications of this type of timesharing service are described in Chapters 4 through 6.
2. **Timesharing services that provide both a library of established programs and a capability for the user to write his own programs on-line.** Utilization of this type of utility service is covered in Chapters 7 through 9.

In general, services in the first category are used to process source transactions and accounting records. Such transactions are normally characterized by large volumes, by standardized formats for the documents involved, and, in some situations, by a substantial degree of uniformity according to the type of business or industry involved.

Timesharing services in the second category are used chiefly for analytical, scientific, engineering, design, or other technical problem-solving tasks. Characteristics of this type of utilization include relatively small volumes, problems of a highly individualized nature, a requirement for mathematically oriented processing, and quantitatively oriented users. With this type of service, the user is most likely to be interested in a single program to solve a specific problem—as distinct from interrelated sets of programs that comprise processing and data file management systems, a characteristic of usage for the first type of utility.

In both types of timesharing service, the processing of user work is handled in the same general manner. Accordingly, the subject of operating-system software and processing techniques is discussed in general terms in the section that follows. There are, however, some significant differences between the two types of timesharing service in the areas of operating controls and file protection, and these aspects of timesharing service utilization are discussed separately in the concluding sections of this chapter.

OPERATING-SYSTEM SOFTWARE

The heart of any timesharing service is its *operating system,* which, as the name suggests, consists of the software that runs the computer—continuously and without human intervention for normal processing. To perform all of the tasks required to run the computer automatically, the operating system needs a number of software elements, including:

- An executive scheduler.
- Configuration control software.
- File handling software.
- A supervisory operator communication system.
- A utilization accounting system.
- Programming-language support.

The Executive Scheduler

Also known as the "supervisor program," the executive scheduler controls the work done by the timesharing computer. This software element continually scans the workload being handled by the central processor. It establishes a lineup, or *queue,* of jobs to be handled. Within the queue, the executive scheduler recognizes codes that assign priorities to jobs in process. It can also reassign, or upgrade, priorities of individual jobs as necessary to move work expeditiously through the computer. For example, most operating-system software automatically upgrades the priority of jobs which have been delayed for the handling of high-priority work. Thus, after a certain number of interruptions, any given job is moved to top priority so that the computer gets all work out within a reasonable time despite interruptions to accommodate special priorities.

The executive scheduler also controls the *swapping* of jobs into and out of the central processor. When a processing delay is encountered, the executive scheduler directs the computer to take out the current program and bring in the next program in the priority queue. In so doing, the executive scheduler designates the file area on a peripheral storage device which will be used for interim retention of the data being processed. The scheduler software also moves programs into and out of its own memory for peripheral retention when they are not being used.

Whenever programs or data being processed are swapped from memory to peripheral storage, the executive scheduling software automatically keeps track of the last instruction processed by establishing and maintaining its own tables for all programs, data files, and work in process. When jobs are swapped out of the central processor, the executive scheduler sets "flags" which keep track of processing status. In other words, when work is interrupted, the executive scheduling software marks its place and assures that it is returned to the queue at the earliest possible time.

Configuration Control

The operating system must maintain accurate records at all times of the status of each element of the computer timesharing system. In many operating systems, the software can actually assign and utilize peripherals or other equipment on its own, without operator intervention. In other cases, the operating system asks the computer operator to assign specific peripherals or other devices according to his particular processing requirements.

The configuration control software reacts automatically when it receives signals indicating that any element of the system is malfunctioning or out of service. Depending on equipment availability, on the severity of an error or malfunction encountered, and on its own capabilities, the configuration control software may react automatically to service interruptions affecting any element of the timesharing system. In some systems, the software can actually reassign peripherals to pick up work which was being handled by units that malfunctioned. In other cases, the operating system simply senses that certain files, programs, or devices are not accessible and processes only those jobs that do not use out-of-service system elements. At any given point, configuration control software operates to achieve the greatest amount of processing that can be performed with the resources available.

File Handling

File handling capabilities and controls assure the validity and integrity of files that are processed automatically. For example, in calling up a program to process a user application input, this software element automatically compares application identification input from the terminal with the label of the file. Designations must correspond or the files cannot be processed.

Similarly, file labels include data on the number of records contained in each file. In the course of processing, new records may be added, two or more records may be merged, and so on. The file handling software must keep track of the impact on file control labels of all processing performed. At the end of each operating function, labels must be validated and updated as necessary. Obviously, without such a capability, automatic service to multiple users could not take place.

File-handling software also applies controls that assure the privacy of user data stored within the timesharing system. This aspect of timesharing utilization is discussed in the section on "Controls," later in this chapter.

Supervisory Operator Communication

All computer systems, no matter how automated, need human support. The supervisory operator communication element of the operating system performs several necessary functions relating to continuity of service. In most timesharing systems, communication is accomplished through messages printed on a console typewriter. In some systems, messages are also displayed on a cathode-ray-tube (CRT) terminal for operator intervention. Emergency communication generally takes the form of the computer ringing bells or blowing loud horns to indicate a serious malfunction.

One subject of continuing communication between the timesharing operating system and the central computer is *status information*. In general, any time a user "signs on" to a timesharing system, a status message will be printed out for the supervisory operator. In addition, the software will also trigger intermittent messages describing the workload currently being handled by the computer system.

Another continuing requirement for communication between the system and the supervisory operator is *setup instructions*. This operating-system element triggers the generation of messages any time special forms must be mounted on a printer, cards entered into a reader or punch, tapes or disk packs mounted, and so on. In addition, the same software controls the triggering of signals and/or messages to the operator whenever any portion of the timesharing system malfunctions.

Naturally, there must also be a capability for receiving and acting upon messages from the supervisory operator to the computer. The operator, for example, may intervene to *change priorities* of various programs. The operator may also *reconfigure the system* or *reassign peripherals*. If a system is overloaded, the operator can enter an instruction that will cause the communication processor to refuse to accept new user jobs until the condition has subsided.

Obviously, the supervisory operator must also *respond to requests* from the computer. If, for example, an instruction has been received to mount invoice forms on a high-speed printer, the operator uses his console typewriter to let the operating system know that the device has been set up and is ready to receive the output.

Utilization Accounting

This element of the operating system keeps track of the time at which each terminal is connected to and disconnected from the system. It also accounts for the amount of central processor time utilized by each program executed.

This software also keeps track of the amount of peripheral storage space assigned to each user. These data, obviously, provide the basis for billing users of the timesharing system.

Programming-Language Support

In those timesharing services that offer on-line programming capabilities to users, programming-language support is essential. One of the keys to the utilization of such timesharing services is to make it possible for the user to write his programs easily, with as much support as possible from the computer itself. The controls that make programming-language capabilities available to the user must be incorporated in the operating system. The actual programming-language software, however, forms a separate element of the timesharing system.

The various types of programming languages and their use are dealt with elsewhere in this book.

PREPROGRAMMED APPLICATION SYSTEMS

Preprogrammed application systems are designed essentially to support the record-keeping function within user companies. The emphasis in such systems is on using the computer to help generate business documents and/or to process routine business transactions. This entire segment of the timesharing service industry is based on the fact that many businesses have transaction patterns and formats in common. Systems are designed in the belief that the operations of many distribution companies, for example, can use similar order, invoicing, shipping, accounts payable, and other documents. Similarly, systems are designed to provide general-purpose manufacturing support documentation, such as bills of material listings, job tickets, labor distributions, and job cost reports.

Obviously, the key to success for such services is the homogeneity of the market segments to which the timesharing utilities are offering their services. By mass-marketing standardized application systems, the timesharing utilities spread the cost of systems design and programming, reducing costs to individual users. At the same time, the user must recognize that a timesharing system of this kind will seldom provide capabilities specially tailored to his operations and management needs. Rather, the user must adapt his needs and goals to the programming packages available—at least to some extent—in order to realize the benefits of preprogrammed timesharing application systems.

A general characteristic of this type of system is that user input is limited to functional commands and data. The programs perform set processing sequences only. Unless the user undertakes or commissions the development of special programs—at comparatively high additional cost— he will have no impact on the system's capabilities. The company utilizing a preprogrammed timesharing application system does so only after weighing the tradeoffs between available capabilities and comparative costs of performing the record-keeping functions in other ways.

USER-PROGRAMMABLE SYSTEMS

User-programmable systems are employed primarily for the problem-solving functions of business management. These include such management tasks as financial projections, financial analyses, modeling, and scheduling.

To do this type of work on a timesharing computer, the user must have access to programming-language software which makes it possible to prepare tailored application programs. In general, timesharing systems use programming languages that are user-oriented, making it possible to bring individual programs into operation with a minimal investment in both management time and out-of-pocket cost.

Programming languages are made available to users through software elements known as *compilers* or *language translators*. This software derives its name from the fact that it compiles, or performs a translation function, to generate binary-level instructions needed to process data on the computer.

The user actually enters his program instructions in what is known as a "high-level format." Different software compilers or language translators are oriented toward the natural communication tendencies of different types of users. Some compilers accept instructions in English-type statements. Others are mathematically oriented, accepting algebraic statements as their instruction set. In either case, the software accepts the user instructions and causes the computer to generate its own binary-level, highly detailed programs.

Some timesharing software language compilers also interact with terminal users. As individual instructions are entered, program segments are generated in machine language to determine the validity and acceptability of the user instructions. If the user has made an erroneous entry, the timesharing software analyzes the error and produces a diagnostic message which serves as the basis for the correction of entries by the user.

Such diagnostic capabilities, understandably, are limited to the area of technical acceptability of the statements for computer processing. The timesharing compilers are said to look for errors in syntax, rather than logic. *Syntax* is a linguistic term describing the grammatic-type validity of programming-language statements. Correct syntax assures that the computer will accept the user statement, generate the appropriate instructions, and perform the processing indicated. The computer, however, has only limited capability for detecting errors in processing *logic*. Thus, with most timesharing systems, it remains possible for the user to prepare valid programs that produce invalid data. This is a built-in hazard of any type of computer programming.

Detailed descriptions and specific evaluations of programming languages available for timesharing users are beyond the scope of this book. However, examples of some commonly used language applications are illustrated in Chapters 8 and 9.

As they have gained experience, most timesharing utility services have found it profitable to build up what are referred to as "libraries" of commonly encountered problem-solving programs. For example, a number of timesharing utilities have noted that their users have required random-number generators for statistical sampling and market analysis applications. Most utilities offering user-programmable capabilities now offer random-number generators as part of a library of program routines that the user can call upon through entry of simplified commands.

Program libraries of problem-solving applications have also been built along industry lines. For example, a number of time-sharing utilities offer programs that automatically calculate depreciation schedules for fixed assets or amortization tables for mortgage loans.

CONTROLS

Controls are particularly critical in a timesharing utility system because the user gives up a measure of custody for his data and business records. With record-keeping applications, information vital to the conduct of the user's business is stored at the time-sharing facility. With problem-solving applications, the user may be storing highly confidential management forecasts and other information on an external computer system. To provide the necessary degree of protection, a timesharing utility should have three levels, or types, of controls, each reliably applied:

1. User access controls.
2. User data controls.
3. System-level protection.

User Access Controls

The "watchdogs" of a timesharing utility system, user access controls determine who may enter the system and what he may do once he gains access. These controls are important to users because they serve to limit the utilization of timesharing computer services on the basis of management-established needs, and also to protect users against erroneous charges for unauthorized use. Access controls differ for preprogrammed and user-programmable timesharing utility systems.

In preprogrammed systems, the first level of access control occurs when the user announces himself. The user enters the company name and, as appropriate, an account number assigned by the timesharing utility. This information is static. It does not change as long as the user remains a customer.

A secondary level of access control is necessary. These controls must have a measure of user discretion or user-applied protection. One method of second-level identification is built into systems where user terminals are hard-wired to leased lines. In such systems, it is possible simply to build identification coding into terminals and communication controllers at the user site. Access to the terminals can then be controlled with locks and keys.

In "dial-up" access systems, passwords are used. These are identification codes that are changed frequently in collaboration between users and timesharing companies. Typically, passwords are changed at irregular intervals from two weeks to one month. The dates of change are varied to prevent unauthorized users from predicting patterns for this type of access control.

Where multiple-application systems have been integrated on a preprogrammed basis, an added level of control can be achieved by assigning separate passwords to individual subsystems. For example, it is possible to create a separate password for a payroll subsystem and for an accounts receivable subsystem. Thus clerical personnel responsible for processing orders cannot gain access to payroll files.

In user-programmable systems, virtually all access is through dial-up lines. Thus hard-wired terminal identification is usually not viable. As with systems offering preprogrammed services, the initial level of identification is the company name and/or account number.

At the next level, this type of timesharing service generally has a user-initiated password. A user who enters confidential data into a timesharing system can change the password as frequently as he feels necessary, possibly several times a day.

In addition, user-programmable systems typically have an extra, or third, level of access control. This is a project code identification assigned by the user. In addition to applying access controls by coding individual projects, the user can generally stipulate that he wishes his billing broken down to the project level for his own cost accounting purposes.

Both types of timesharing service use techniques that obliterate, or do not print, passwords on printed records created at user terminals. This is done either by striking over passwords after they have been entered or, on equipment where this is feasible, by suppressing the printing function completely when the computer system asks the user for the password. The password is entered, but confidentiality is maintained by eliminating readable entries at the terminal.

User Data Controls

User data controls are designed to protect both the privacy and the integrity of files maintained on timesharing systems. Two types of file protection are necessary:

1. **Protection against unauthorized access.** This can occur at two levels. First, there must be protection to assure that users do not gain access to each other's files. Second, there must be techniques that prevent unauthorized personnel within a user company from gaining access to files they are not supposed to see.
2. **Protection against accidental destruction of files.** This would occur as a result of authorized users committing errors.

There are five techniques that can be applied to protect user files: file label controls, ciphering, binary-only storage, random-access keys, and read-only files.

File Label Controls. Each file within a timesharing system should contain a user account number. Each file access operation should validate a correspondence between user transaction codes and file identification to protect against unauthorized external access to data. This is the highest level of protection for user files, since it is incorporated into basic software for the utility system. This type of control is applied universally, to all transactions, over and above the discretion of the individual user.

Ciphering. Some timesharing utilities offering user-programmable service permit the user to designate a cipher code that protects his file against unauthorized access. The ciphering technique protects against both access from unauthorized personnel within the user company and access to the files by employees of the computer utility itself. To utilize this technique, the user makes up his own cipher code according to a format made available by the utility. However, the individual user keeps this code to himself.

When the cipher is entered, the computer processes it under an algorithmic formula that scrambles file content into nonsensical patterns. When data are to be accessed, the algorithm must first be applied to uncipher the data. In general, this technique, the most sophisticated available for protection against unauthorized access, is applied only to the most confidential files. Its use is restricted by the extra cost of the processing time needed to execute the cipher algorithm for both input and reference transactions.

Binary-Only Storage.   A second level of protection against unauthorized access by company employees can be applied, in some utility systems, by instructing the computer to store data in binary format only—rather than in characters or numbers. This approach makes it possible to enter and access data directly, eliminating the cost of processing the cipher algorithm. Protection exists because most people cannot conveniently translate binary coding into meaningful file content.

Random-Access Keys.   This control, a third level of protection against unauthorized access, is applied to the very location of records on data files. The access key is an algorithmic formula for locating data on random-access files. For example, a series of calculations may be applied to customer numbers or inventory item numbers in order to find the needed records. User control is achieved because the access formula is contained within the user program. Thus users must be able to gain access to specific programs before they can use the associated data files.

Even if file content is called out of a timesharing system in an unauthorized manner, this technique will scramble the order in which records are presented. However, since anyone with normal access to the application can call up these data, this is the lowest level of file protection.

Read-Only Files.   Read-only files are a technique for protecting users against their own errors. Files within a timesharing system can be coded so that users can only read them—that is, they cannot alter their content. The most common use of the read-only technique is for protection of user programs in a user-programmable system. In addition, the user will frequently designate for read-only storage data files that have been developed only after extensive processing.

Within a preprogrammed system, the timesharing utility itself will generally protect its programs against user intervention or alteration through the read-only technique.

System-Level Protection

System-level protection measures guard against destruction of data through accident to or malfunction of either the computer itself or communication equipment within the timesharing system. Three techniques are used to achieve this objective:

1. System reconstruction.
2. Equipment redundancy.
3. Alternate off-line procedures.

The first technique should be applied universally by all time-sharing utlities. The second is rarely used. The third technique applies to preprogrammed application systems only.

System Reconstruction. System reconstruction includes methods for rebuilding files of data and programs that may be destroyed either accidentally or through computer malfunctions—such as head crashes on disk files. Two interrelated techniques are commonly used. One calls for use of magnetic-tape files to log all transactions processed by the timesharing system. Frequently, two tape drives are used for logging, providing an additional measure of protection. (Although log tapes provide a record of transactions processed during the day, they do not indicate which files have been accessed during the day.)

Direct-access files are protected through a technique known as a "system dump." To illustrate, when disk files are used for direct-access storage, the file content is simply copied from one pack to another, or to magnetic tape, at preestablished times. This is usually done on a daily basis, as part of the normal maintenance cycle—if possible, when the system is out of service.

If an on-line file should be destroyed, both the system and log files are used for reconstruction. The system dump file corresponds with the status of the data for the previous period or processing day. The log indicates transactions processed during the current day. All timesharing utilities have reconstruction programs and procedures that process the current day's transaction log against the previous day's dump to reconstruct on-line files on a current basis. Generally, at least three days of file dumps and logs are maintained for reconstruction backup. These are generally referred to as "grandfather," "father," and "son" files.

This level of protection should be built into all record-keeping systems offered by timesharing utilities. Some utilities providing user-programmable services, however, protect with file dumps only; they do not log transactions. In such cases, the user should maintain records of each day's transactions, usually by saving the printout on his terminal. If on-line files are destroyed within such systems, it becomes the responsibility of the user to provide the transactions necessary to update the previous day's dump.

The presence of system dump files offers potential protection for users of systems with programming options who may inadvertently erase their own files. Should this happen, the previous day's dump may be used to reconstruct erased files on a selective basis up to the present day's entries.

Equipment Redundancy. Some timesharing systems—though not many operated by utility companies—use multiple computers as backup protection against interruption of service. This approach calls for availability of identical central processors, and of some peripheral devices that can be switched between processors. Then, if one processor fails, the second can be activated. The same, of course, applies to alternate peripheral devices.

As indicated, not many timesharing utilities provide this level of protection. Therefore, in considering timesharing services, the user should acquire estimates of the probability of service interruptions and evaluate their consequences for his own operations.

Alternate Off-Line Procedures. If a timesharing utility is used to process transactions vital to the continuity of a company's business, alternate, manual procedures should be established for use at times when service is interrupted. For example, a savings and loan association which has its accounting processed on a timesharing computer should have a method of handling customer transactions off-line. Typically this is done by installing terminals that can post customer passbooks electromechanically, independently of the computer. When service is interrupted, transactions are handled normally, with entries made on a journal tape posted by the machine and coded to indicate that these entries have not been made into the computer files. Then, when service is restored, the affected transactions can be entered and processed.

Such backup procedures require extensive documentation from the computer utility. In the on-line savings application, for example, the institution generally receives complete trial balances of accounts each day. Thus tellers can process deposits routinely but refer to printed computer output reports for withdrawal authorizations.

Similarly, a distribution company processing invoices on a timesharing utility should have a method for continuing to do business through manual document preparation and later entry of data into computer files if service is interrupted.

Obviously, this requirement applies only for preprogrammed, record-keeping systems.

4 General
Accounting
Applications

The general accounting applications described in this chapter were among the earliest timesharing services available to business management, and over the years these applications have continued to represent a substantial and dynamic part of the timesharing service market. New developments in data communication techniques and terminal equipment leave little room for doubt that accounting and record-keeping uses of computer timesharing services will continue to expand rapidly in the foreseeable future.

THE NATURE OF
GENERAL ACCOUNTING APPLICATIONS

Broadly defined, general accounting applications include the entire spectrum of financially significant transactions conducted by a business. Two key characteristics of such applications are (1) a relatively large volume of transactions and (2) procedures and documentation formats that lend themselves to the degree of standardization required for the economical use of preprogrammed timesharing services.

Individual applications in the general accounting area tend to correspond with the subsystems of a company's general ledger accounting system:

- Order entry and invoicing.
- Accounts receivable.
- Inventory record-keeping.
- Accounts payable/cash disbursements.

44

- Payroll.
- Job cost/labor distribution.
- General journal entries.

The cumulative effect of processing all or most of these trans-actions through a typical business-oriented timesharing system is to create a computerized general ledger file—or at least a com-puterized file that represents a substantial part of the company's general ledger. Since the user has on-line access to this file, it can also serve as a data base for management information inquiries. This management inquiry capability has, in fact, proved to be a major consideration in many companies' decisions to use a time-sharing system (rather than off-line accounting machines, in-house batch computer systems, or batch-processing service bureaus) for their general accounting applications.

ADVANTAGES OF TIMESHARING

The advantages and benefits of using a timesharing system for general accounting and record-keeping include the following:

- Management information inquiry capabilities are available as an inexpensive by-product of the routine processing of necessary business transactions.
- The inherent efficiency of exception processing becomes avail-able because of the on-line file reference capabilities of such systems. In a conventional invoicing system, for example, processing follows assembly-line patterns. First credit must be checked, then ordered items must frequently be checked against separate inventory record files. With an on-line computer, these references are handled automatically and in fractions of a second. Management need concern itself only with the exception situations identified by the computer.
- A capability for producing accurate, validated documents quickly is part of most business timesharing systems. Under one of the systems described later in this chapter, for ex-ample, an accounts payable check can be written on a com-puter terminal in a matter of seconds to comply with C.O.D.

receiving situations. Under another system, invoices are written as a by-product of the capturing of order information.

- For appropriate applications, the speed and efficiency of on-line timesharing systems are equal to or better than those of other data-processing techniques available at comparable cost.
- Work volumes or application areas can be expanded with relative ease—and without commensurate increases in the cost of equipment and programming.
- Some timesharing utilities offering general accounting services bill customers entirely on the basis of the number of transactions processed. Under this approach, the cost of the service varies directly with the volume of business. For the user this can represent a significant advantage in comparison with a fee schedule based on terminal connect time, central processor time, or a combination of both. The transaction-charge approach makes it possible, in effect, for a user company to have the timesharing computer at its disposal all the time. In some situations, the terminals are actually connected to the system throughout the business day, but the user is charged only for the actual transactions processed.
- The costly and time-consuming handling of errors or out-of-balance conditions that occurs with batch processing—in either a service bureau or an in-house installation—is significantly reduced through on-line timesharing service. This is because exception instructions are identified and corrected as they occur.

SOME WORDS OF CAUTION

There are some limitations to, and potential problems associated with, the use of timesharing services of which prospective users should be aware. The following areas, especially, should be considered carefully before a decision is made to use timesharing services for the company's general accounting applications:

- Costs, as always, need to be considered carefully and, along with benefits, compared with those of alternative approaches.

In addition to the usage-based cost of the timesharing utility service, other elements of cost include the purchase or rental of terminal equipment, leasing of communication lines in some situations, and a basic charge for subscription to the timesharing service (including the setting up of a dedicated portal into the computer system).

- The company must conform its document formats and procedures to those built into the system. This can impose both design and functional limitations on documents, transactions, and information files.
- The user may experience interruptions in service from the timesharing utility in situations that can be unpredictable and beyond his control. Malfunctions of either the computer or the communication links can deprive a user of computer access at crucial times. Therefore, to apply such a system effectively, the user company must have backup procedures that are brought into effect with reduced efficiency and control when the timesharing system is down.
- Custody of company data is delegated to an outside vendor. The same considerations apply here as when service bureaus are used. The user company must establish and maintain backup files—and must be sure that reports generated by the timesharing system assure an adequate level of operating continuity for the company.

THE KEY ISSUE: COMPATIBILITY

Compatibility between the capabilities of a timesharing system and the day-to-day operations of the user company is a must. Both commitment and adaptation are necessary on both sides. The matchup of a timesharing company and a user has, with some justification, been likened to a marriage. The timesharing system must, for its part, be adaptable to the patterns and customs of the user's business. But, obviously, there are limits to the extent of adaptation that can be accomplished. No one system can ever be an ideal fit for every user.

On the other side, the user must be ready to operate its business with support systems that are something less than optimal. A company, for example, may have to revise some of its business forms to fit the output patterns of a timesharing computer service. Similarly, the content of information files or timetables for management reports may have to be adapted to fit the preestablished schedules of the timesharing utility.

As a basis for individual decisions, it is possible to develop a checklist of points at which the probable compatibility of a particular user company and a timesharing service can be measured and evaluated to determine whether, in fact, a marriage will be workable. In evaluating these points of compatibility, management of the user company should be just as wary as an individual contemplating matrimony.

At the present time—and this seems likely to hold true for the immediate future—it is the user who makes the more binding commitment. The user company almost always agrees to alter its customs and procedures to some extent. The user changes its way of doing things, impacting both its employees and its relationships with customers. Even though a timesharing service may seem easily cancelable, the cost of conversion, of doing things differently for even a little while, will inevitably lead to problems if the timesharing system does not work out well for the user.

At least five points at which compatibility should be evaluated can be identified. These are listed below in the order of their importance in achieving compatibility between the user company and the timesharing utility:

1. The number of items of data that the system will allow the user to capture in processing each transaction.
2. The level of detail on user files that will be carried, supported, and protected by the system and made available to the user.
3. The account coding structure required for system input and file maintenance.
4. The levels at which data summarization is normally performed by the system.
5. The scheduling and frequency of reports delivered by the system.

Data Per Transaction

The amount of data a user can enter into the system for processing as part of an individual transaction bears directly on the compatibility of the system with the user company's business. This can be illustrated by some simple examples. Suppose a company has procedures that require the entering of a discount rate for each order processed; if the timesharing utility's program permits only a set schedule of discounts within a reference file table, there may not be enough range of percentages to take in all of the user's requirements. Or, in another situation, a user may establish different discounts for each line item processed on an order for one customer; if the timesharing program is restricted to one discount rate for the entire order, problems might arise.

In considering this compatibility factor, the user should give attention to two elements of service expected from the timesharing system. One is whether transaction information entered by the user would exist within the computer system in usable form for any further processing required by the user company. The other consideration is whether the information supporting individual transactions is retrievable by the user.

The question of usability might seem obvious. But the user should be sure to follow through to determine that the computer system can, in fact, handle any transactions that are likely to occur in the conduct of his business—particularly those transactions that occur occasionally but regularly. A timesharing system that can handle 80 percent of a company's transactions for a given application may actually be of no value because of the extra work required to process the remaining 20 percent on an exception basis.

Similarly, the ability to retrieve information entered into a computer system could become critical in controlling and validating transactions basic to the company's operations. If a user cannot verify transactions entered into the system through recall of data, the system may not be workable for that particular company—or the company may require or have to investigate alternate, compensating controls.

The amount of data that can be entered in an individual transaction also affects the ultimate usefulness of a timesharing system to user management. For example, if a system does not permit entry of a sales territory code with customer orders, sales analysis through processing of application files could be difficult.

Level of File Detail

The degree of detail in which data are stored in retrievable format—coupled with retention schedules within files for individual levels of detail—is an important consideration in determining the compatibility and value of a timesharing system to a particular user organization. One example would be a determination of whether a timesharing system retains customer orders in the form in which they are entered or whether the data are broken down in other files immediately upon entry. If customer orders are retained, the length of retention schedules could affect the value of these data for the user company.

Similarly, the level of detail of files that support general ledger applications can affect both management utilization of a system and end-of-year auditing procedures. Typically, all transactions processed by a timesharing system are captured first in a general journal format. These are posted, and may to some extent be summarized, within the general ledger files—usually on a monthly basis—creating a highly desirable level of detail within a general ledger. However, under some systems, the detail within general ledger accounts is cleared out of computer files shortly after monthly general ledger reports are created. Thus, at year-end a company has 12 separate "little" general ledgers rather than one fully computerized base of general ledger data for year-end processing and analysis.

The usefulness of files created by a timesharing system may be affected, as far as the user is concerned, if purged files are retained in some machine-readable form. For example, suppose a timesharing system does purge its general ledger files after monthly reports are issued. A high degree of later usability can be retained if these purged records are read onto magnetic tape and stored by the timesharing utility—rather than being eliminated entirely when they are removed from the on-line file. Thus, if the data were retained on magnetic tape, it would be possible at year-end to reenter the monthly data and produce a comprehensive general ledger report covering all activities of the 12-month period.

Obviously, then, the level of detail of a timesharing utility's files should be analyzed in the light of relatively long-range company information needs.

Account Coding Structure

The account coding structure within the timesharing system must be both compatible with and able to support the established breakdowns in the company's chart of accounts. The computer system itself should be able to recognize and react to significant digit positions within a chart of accounts—for both major and minor account groupings.

Should a timesharing system require a change in the company's chart of accounts, the work and cost associated with conversion from present methods will be far greater and more complex than if compatibility exists. In addition, many companies' charts of accounts conform to either government or industry reporting specifications, and for such companies compatibility on the part of the timesharing system is critical.

The capacity available for account coding is also important. Specifically, there should be enough digital positions available to encode all of a company's subsidiary ledger accounts. For example, companies commonly break down subsidiary ledgers to provide specific identification for individual customers, vendors, employees, and so on. In addition, the capacity of the timesharing system's account coding structure should be evaluated in light of the company's growth projections.

At the risk of belaboring the obvious, it is worth repeating that the accounting systems offered by a particular timesharing utility should be compatible with the accounting methods of the prospective user. As noted above, compatibility with the chart of accounts is especially important.

Level of Data Summarization

The level at which files are summarized within a timesharing system has an important bearing on the value that can be derived from the system's management inquiry capability. Typically, a company's operating management has two primary interests: exception conditions and status information. Exception conditions should be reported routinely as a by-product of transaction processing. Status information should be available through reference to summarizations of user files.

Examples of summary-level references are order volumes on a daily basis, order volumes according to salesmen, accounts receivable aged by due date, overdue accounts receivable by territory, cash on hand, and so on. In general, management requests for summary information fall into two categories as far as computer processing of these inquiries is concerned: (1) requests for figures that exist in summary form within computer files normally and routinely, and (2) requests that require reprocessing of detailed data and development of summary figures.

Obviously, the closer the match between the summary-level files normally retained by a timesharing system and user inquiry patterns, the better.

Reporting Schedules

Reporting schedules are the least important area of concern as regards compatibility between timesharing systems and user companies. However, all users of business timesharing systems require some off-line reporting on a regular basis. These reports provide both operating and backup data for user management. Since these reports are produced off-line at the computer center itself, their cost is significantly less than would be experienced if the same data were generated by an on-line terminal. Thus the frequency, format, and usefulness of such reports to company executives bears directly on the value of a timesharing system to a user company.

EXAMPLES OF TIMESHARING SERVICES

The nature of the services typically provided by timesharing utilities for general accounting applications can be illustrated by citing as examples two successful organizations, which we shall identify as Utility X and Utility Y.

Utility X

Utility X, established in the early 1960s, is an acknowledged pioneer in business timesharing. The company's primary "product" has been an on-line order entry/invoicing system with real-time inventory control capabilities. Located in the population-saturated Northeast Corridor, Utility X has been able to build a clientele of some 350 companies, chiefly in wholesaling and distribution.

At this writing, the great majority of Utility X users have special-configuration terminals utilizing two teletypewriters. However, a high-speed, multipurpose terminal has been announced and is expected to be introduced in the immediate future. In the typical user installation, one teletypewriter is a printer only; the other, equipped with a standard teletypewriter keyboard, serves as both a printer and a data entry unit.

With the Utility X service, the operator, working at the teletypewriter keyboard, enters coded information from the user company's own order forms. Only numeric codes need be entered. The initial entry, for example, is the customer number. On the basis of this, the computer causes the teletypewriter to print in complete invoice heading data, including special shipping instructions as appropriate.

Then, for each line item ordered, the operator enters the item code and quantity. The computer then causes the teletypewriter to print out an item description, unit cost, and extended price, applying discount schedules as appropriate. At the same time that the line-item data are being typed on the invoice, the second teletypewriter, equipped with a dual-feed platen, is typing picking labels for the needed merchandise. The system is capable of creating individual picking labels for each case ordered if the user's business requires this level of supporting detail.

Also on the second teletypewriter is a continuous journal sheet that is used to report exception information on inventories of ordered items. The computer automatically reduces available inventory quantities as order amounts are processed. When any transaction brings inventory levels to reorder points established by users, or to out-of-stock conditions, a message is typed on this register.

Utility X services include regular reporting on inventory status, "open to buy" reports on low-stock items, accounts receivable summaries, and sales analysis reports. To this basic application package, the company has added what could be classified as limited general ledger support subsystems. One of the more logically integrated of these is an accounts payable reporting capability which closes the loop between the order processing system and inventory replenishment.

Utility Y

Utility Y, which was established some years later than Utility X, has achieved its success by developing a broader-based user services package. This approach has been aimed at building a sustaining volume of business in the less densely populated Los Angeles market. Like Utility X, Utility Y offers an order entry/invoicing system. In Y, however, this service is viewed as a building block for a more extensive system rather than as a separate "package." Utility Y's order entry/invoicing system feeds directly into an extensive general ledger system, and the service is marketed accordingly as an "interactive accounting system." Also feeding into the general ledger system are several other subsystems that function at the same level as the order entry/invoicing system:

- Payroll, including a capability for loading checks into a general-purpose terminal and writing them on-line.
- Accounts receivable, including statement-writing capabilities for manufacturers or service companies.
- Work-in-process reporting for manufacturers, including job cost reporting capabilities.
- Contract status reporting of the type used by small manufacturers supplying the aerospace industry.

Utility Y's order entry/invoicing subsystem functions along the same general lines as the Utility X system described above. Under Y's approach, however, the terminal is not dedicated to a single application—that is, the order clerk can use the terminal for inventory status, credit, or other subsystem inquiries on a continuing basis. Then, when an invoice is to be written, an invoice form is inserted into the terminal. Many users, however, write only

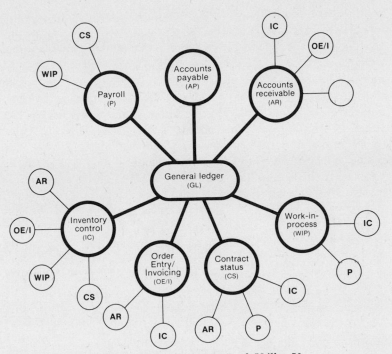

Figure 4.1 "Interactive accounting system" of Utility Y.

high-priority or emergency invoices on their terminals; most of the invoices and picking lists are prepared on high-speed printers at the computer center and delivered to users the following morning by messenger.

For the most part, marketing emphasis for the Y system has been on the comprehensiveness of the general ledger capability and its attendant management inquiry benefits. The relationship between the general ledger 'and application subsystems within Utility Y's "interactive accounting system" is illustrated schematically in Figure 4.1.

MANAGEMENT VALUES

Management values are the key to timesharing feasibility for many users—particularly small companies and divisions of larger organizations. Basically, the decision to use timesharing services for general accounting applications calls for a choice of this approach over a wide variety of semiautomatic and electronic techniques available on a stand-alone basis. In many situations, a minicomputer or electronic accounting machine could handle routine transaction processing as quickly and economically as a timesharing terminal. The deciding factor in such instances is the value of being able to use computer files as an easily accessible source of management and operating information.

The value of this kind of management inquiry capability is illustrated well by a situation in which a timesharing computer is used to allocate cash resources within an accounts payable system. Where an integrated on-line system is available, a manager can interrogate both the cash and accounts payable files to determine whether there is sufficient cash on hand to liquidate all presently due accounts payable invoices—and to retain a minimal cash reserve for other operating requirements. If the system indicates that cash on hand is insufficient for all outstanding invoices, the manager can request a report summarizing those invoices that can be paid through a given due date. The same report will also inform the manager of the amount of discounts that will be lost through failure to pay the remaining invoices on a timely basis. On the basis of this information, the manager can instruct the computer to project the effect of first paying all invoices with discounts available, regardless of their due date. If the manager chooses this course, the system will allocate available funds to discountable invoices first. The remaining funds will then be allocated on the basis of due date, the oldest being paid first. This analysis will also tell the manager the due date for the oldest outstanding invoice that would remain unpaid if he chose this approach. Once the manager selects the alternative he wishes to follow, the system generates checks automatically.

Another illustration of the kind of value that management can derive from the use of timesharing services is in the area of credit followup reports. Typically, a timesharing service will issue aged trial balances on a monthly basis for all of the user company's customers. One system is programmed to print telephone numbers and customer contact names for all accounts showing balances more than 60 days old.

The availability of credit information on-line can also be important. Suppose, for example, that a customer places an order that is considerably larger than usual, for an amount that exceeds its established credit limits. The manager concerned can immediately inquire into the timesharing system to produce reports on sales volumes, payment history, and the current status of this account. Such information, obviously, will play an important part in the manager's decision of how to handle this transaction.

Under some systems, personnel data on employees can be included in payroll files. Thus, in searching for people to fill special assignments or vacant jobs, managers can prepare a profile of their requirements and derive a list of those employees who appear to have the stipulated qualifications.

Manufacturing companies using timesharing systems can develop performance reports based on productivity data accumulated in the computer files. Obviously, the availability of sales data by customer and territory can be an important tool in both sales analysis and sales management.

Timesharing systems can be especially valuable for companies that operate out of multiple locations. A number of companies use timesharing systems instead of establishing multiple data-processing capabilities precisely to gain this advantage. With timesharing, each branch or local office can process its own transactions yet accumulate a data file that can be interrogated by the headquarters office for a current reading on the state of the business.

Given soundly organized files arranged to achieve an adequate degree of compatibility between the user and the timesharing service, potential management uses of the summarized data available from a timesharing system are limited only by the imagination and aggressiveness of individual managers.

5 Special Industry Applications

Not all marriages between companies using timesharing services for business record-keeping applications and the utilities offering such services are subject to the limitations and potential problems described in Chapter 4. A situation with all of the ingredients for a perfect match exists in a growing number of industries with characteristics that lend themselves to uniformity of transaction formats and information reporting.

The "naturalness" of this timesharing market can be illustrated dramatically by one of its prime success stories—the use of timesharing services for on-line transaction processing by savings and loan associations and savings banks.

A NATURAL MARKET: THE SAVINGS INDUSTRY

Both savings and loan associations and savings banks are regulated institutions providing specific, approved services on a basis of mandated uniformity. Marketing in these industries is concerned largely with convenience and intangible personal services. The actual transactions associated with the main businesses of these institutions—savings accounts and mortgage loans—are uniform in terms of both allowable interest rates and the nature of the services to which customers are entitled. Even optional services, such as Christmas clubs or vacation clubs, tend to be highly uniform.

The concept of on-line processing of savings account transactions originated in Eastern metropolitan areas, where savings institutions experience extremely heavy customer traffic. The institution generally credited with initiating this type of service is the Dime Savings Bank, headquartered in Brooklyn, New York. As early as 1964, this institution had scores of branches scattered throughout the New York City area, each open six days a week, some with special, late hours and/or unusual locations. A number of branches, for example, were located in subway stations.

In these and other savings institutions in Eastern metropolitan areas, depositors typically visit their local branch every week, to cash their paycheck and deposit a small portion of their earnings. Typically, more than half of each day's volume of transactions is handled during the lunch hour. Things become particularly frantic during interest-posting periods—the first ten days of each quarter—when many depositors stop by routinely to have accumulated interest posted in their passbooks.

Interbranch transactions have also been growing in volume and significance in this industry. Typically, a customer will establish an account in a branch near his or her home, but frequently use the branch closest to his or her place of employment to make deposits, withdraw money, or cash checks.

Not long after on-line systems were initiated, a new service concept swept the savings industry that put a premium value on fast turnaround in transaction processing: the computing and payment of interest to depositors on a "compounded daily" basis. Now, any time a depositor either withdrew money or demanded an accounting for his or her interest, the current annual rate had to be computed on a daily basis for the entry.

Traditional record-keeping and transaction-processing methods among savings institutions were simply not able to keep pace with the growth in the volume and complexity of transactions faced by the industry. Records for individual depositors or lenders were maintained on separate ledger. cards. As a basis for each transaction posting, the teller had to enter the old balance for the account. This in turn served as a basis for updating the account through window posting machines with simple addition and subtraction capabilities. On the all-too-frequent occasions when the old-balance pickup was erroneous, the current account status was also fallacious. Interest calculations still had to be performed by hand. A number of institutions had installed punched-card accounting and batch computer systems to handle account posting on an overnight basis. These systems expedited the processing of deposits, but they were of no help at all in the processing of withdrawals or the cashing of checks.

In a case that shocked the industry shortly before the installation of on-line systems, savings institutions in a single Eastern city were bilked of approximately $250,000 during one week by a syndicate of confidence men who established accounts with worthless out-of-town checks, then withdrew the funds a week later. These withdrawals were timed carefully to occur after new-account "holds" had been dropped but before the deposited checks had bounced.

CHARACTERISTICS OF A NATURAL INDUSTRY MARKET

The characteristics that make an industry a natural market for specialized timesharing services are easy to identify:

1. The industry has a relatively large number of users with uniform transaction and information-reporting formats. Individual users may experience comparatively low volumes, but collectively they constitute a significant market.
2. Regulations or other requirements for uniformity make it practical for large numbers of users to buy uniform services. Savings institutions have already been cited as an illustration. Another example is automotive dealers who have contractual obligations to provide uniform parts inventory reporting and ordering input to the factories that supply them.
3. A dollar value can be placed on the immediacy of response available from an on-line timesharing system.
4. The volume of business represented by the industry makes it possible for timesharing utilities to develop fee structures that are highly competitive with the costs of stand-alone systems which users can operate independently.

Many industries, and many more companies, fit this profile, and their number promises to grow. Thus, special-industry applications appear to represent one of the more rapidly expanding markets for timesharing services for some time to come.

OTHER SPECIAL INDUSTRY APPLICATIONS

Some typical industry applications in which specialized timesharing services have found success include utility billing systems, hospital accounting and reporting systems, inventory and other systems for automotive and equipment dealers, on-line reservation systems, and specialized systems for securities dealers and financial institutions. Each of these applications is discussed briefly below.

Utility Billing

Companies providing power, gas, water, or refuse collection services generally enter billing data on a remote batch basis. Typically, documents are marked by field personnel who read meters (except in the case of refuse collection, which is ordinarily handled on a flat-monthly-fee basis) and place marks on grid patterns on reporting forms. These marks are read automatically by document-reading devices. Data can be either transmitted directly to a timesharing computer or accumulated at the user location on punched or magnetic tape. When the data are entered into the timesharing computer, customer files are updated and bills are generated automatically.

A major control value for user companies derives from the ability to credit customer payments on-line. Thus, if a customer comes to a cashier's window, account status is immediately available. Account status information is also immediately available to service dispatchers.

Hospitals

For hospitals, the most urgent single need fulfilled by the timesharing approach is the ability to have current account status information available when patients are discharged. Specialized timesharing services available to hospitals provide capabilities for computing third-party (insurance company or government agency) payments on patient accounts and for accounting for amounts owed by individual patients. Additional benefits derive from the ability of the computer to help account for and control the dispensing of pharmaceuticals, and to develop patient occupancy reports. Increasing numbers of hospitals are also using timesharing systems for budgetary planning programs like the ones described in Chapters 7 and 8.

Automotive and Equipment Dealers

Dealers in automobiles and trucks, farm equipment, and construction machinery are expected to carry current parts inventories that may include from 40,000 to 100,000 different items. Typically, such dealers are signatories to contracts with supplying factories which require that they provide specific levels of service in response to customer demands for parts, that they report on-hand stock status periodically, and that they commit a given dollar amount to inventories. On-line response capability is often valuable in parts sales because business is conducted on an over-the-counter basis.

The actual processing of parts orders and invoices proceeds along the same general lines as those described in the preceding chapter for general-purpose order entry, invoicing, and inventory reporting systems. Of particular interest to such dealers is the receipt of immediate reports on low-stock or out-of-stock status on fast-moving items.

Increasing numbers of automotive dealers are also subscribing to timesharing services offered by either independent utilities or large commercial banks for the interactive processing of retail sales contracts for automobiles. The immediacy of timesharing is especially valuable in this impulse-buying market. With available timesharing systems, the dealer can compute effective interest rates and determine exact amounts of monthly payments, including optional life insurance coverage on the amount of the loan. The dealer is now in a position to guarantee the monthly payment to the customer at the moment of highest interest in the purchase. In situations where the bank will have credit recourse to the dealer for the sale, the transaction can be concluded and a car delivered to the customer almost immediately. At the very least, the dealer has the information necessary to write and have the customer sign a valid contract right on the spot.

On-Line Reservations

Following the success of in-house timesharing systems for airline reservations, a number of timesharing utilities have developed "package" services for the sale of other types of tickets—particularly for entertainment and sporting events. This has been done chiefly through special-purpose timesharing terminals installed in retail and other service-oriented outlets.

These applications are relatively straightforward. Data banks are established to represent available seats for given events on specific dates. When a customer inquires about the availability of seats, the attendant asks for a printout that lists vacancies according to price range or location. When the customer makes his selection, the attendant collects the money and activates transaction keys which cause a special-purpose printer within the terminal to produce finished tickets that will be honored for admission to the events covered. At the same time, the timesharing computer updates its inventory of available seats.

Some experimentation has been done with the offering of other facilities or services through such systems, including sightseeing tours and other attractions subject to limited availability.

Securities Dealers

As transaction volumes on the country's securities exchanges have multiplied, dealers in securities have been threatened with paperwork inundation. At this writing, timesharing solutions to the problems of stockbrokers are still largely in the developmental stage. Basically, however, the services currently being offered establish files of open transaction records and associated followup reports to help dealers ensure that securities bought or sold are received from customers and delivered accordingly. The same timesharing system can also establish inventory records for securities maintained in the brokerage firm's own portfolio. When newly purchased securities are received, the system can provide either instructions for mailing or the mailing labels themselves. With timesharing support, the managers of a brokerage firm can determine the status of the business at any time during a trading day.

Financial Institutions

A number of commercial banks have arranged to have their savings account transaction processing handled by the same time-sharing utility services that derive most of their revenue from savings and loan associations and savings banks. In such cases, the utilities have extended their programs to cover the interest rates and other special requirements of the banks.

Similar applications for processing savings and loan accounts have also been made available to a number of employee credit unions. Credit union program packages developed by timesharing utilities include listings provided to employer companies detailing payroll deductions authorized by employees. In a few cases, time-sharing utilities have been able to provide machine-readable media suitable for direct input into company payroll programs. Similarly, some companies have arranged to provide magnetic-tape files on payroll deductions as input for credit union timesharing systems.

For credit unions, a special dimension provided by the use of timesharing services is the control implicit in the use of a reliable outside source. Officers of credit unions assume substantial responsibilities, especially considering that most are volunteers. Also, because of their cooperative nature, credit unions generally prefer to minimize the size of their full-time staff. Timesharing services provide needed support at lower costs than can be achieved manually, and with far greater reliability. In addition, timesharing utilities serving credit unions generally organize the files so that on-line inquiries provide both the savings and the loan status of each member. This is valuable because credit union charters generally require that a certain relationship be maintained between savings accounts and loan accounts.

At this writing, another rapidly growing area of timesharing utility service is the support of central information file (CIF) programs for commercial banks. Under these programs, customer accounts are interrelated through reference tables. An inquiry concerning any customer account produces a report on the user terminal that covers all relations of the bank with that customer, including accounts for which the individual is cosignatory, corporate accounts in which the individual is involved, loans, checking accounts, and savings accounts. In effect, each customer inquiry delivers a complete business profile to the requesting officer. These inquiries will be made to the same files, in many instances, that are used to support batch demand deposit accounting applications processed on an overnight basis.

One timesharing service headquartered in Los Angeles is offering customer banks an option for installing small magnetic ink character recognition (MICR) readers on their own premises. These units capture data on magnetic tape for remote batch transmission to the timesharing service, and the checks themselves never leave the bank. After transmission, the bank can sort the checks itself at relatively slow speeds on its own reader.

HOW THE ON-LINE SAVINGS SYSTEM WORKS

The on-line savings application described at the beginning of this chapter is an excellent illustration of both the principles and the potential benefits associated with special-industry applications of timesharing. A number of organizations—including commercial banks operating on a correspondent basis—have offered timesharing utility services to savings banks and savings and loan associations. In some instances, large savings institutions have offered such services to smaller ones.

For the purposes of illustration, this discussion will describe, at a functional level, the processing performed by one utility offering on-line savings and mortgage services—the data centers operated in a number of cities across the country by The National Cash Register Company (NCR). At this writing, some nine million savings institution accounts are being serviced by NCR centers. Entries are being made from approximately 3300 special-purpose teller window machines. These machines are the only ones compatible with the system. Obviously, sales of these units at prices of more than $4000 each, and of associated communication equipment, have combined to provide a not insignificant incentive for NCR to venture into the specialized timesharing field.

One of the system characteristics that led to rapid acceptance of NCR's on-line procedures among savings institutions was the similarity of these on-line procedures to those that had already become standard throughout most of the industry. In developing a terminal for on-line savings account and mortgage loan processing, NCR entered the field by converting an existing machine, the Class 42 teller window unit, to on-line operation. This was a machine already popular in the industry. For on-line use, the same configuration was modified by the installation of banks of solenoids to activate the keyboard automatically. Communication with the central computer is through a controller for each window machine and a multiplexor in each branch office using the system. The multiplexor, in turn, is able to communicate through a single modem, serving up to 16 machines on a single telephone line.

As was true of the earlier, stand-alone machines, the NCR window machine prints all transaction items, whether they are initiated by the teller or the computer, on a continuous journal tape. If service is interrupted, the machine can still be used off-line, in much the same way that this was done under earlier manual procedures. When off-line entries are made on a teller machine, an identifying cipher is imprinted to call attention to this status. The journal tape can then be used as a basis for reentry of transaction data when computer service is resumed.

To process a savings transaction, the teller still accepts and uses a depositor passbook in time-honored fashion. The machine actually has a sensing device that requires insertion of a passbook—or identification of the transaction as a "no book" item—before processing can begin. The teller enters the account number, which is verified by the computer and posted in the passbook as a control. Then the teller enters the amount and uses descriptor keys to identify the transaction. The computer updates an on-line file for the depositor's account and enters new balance information automatically. If the on-line file shows that interest is due for posting in the customer's passbook, this is done automatically. If no passbook has been presented, a record is set up specifically to post this transaction the next time the depositor's passbook is presented. Another important control feature is that the on-line depositor file is changed to reflect the date of the last transaction affecting each account. Also, if a deposit is keyed into the system as a check, the computer will automatically encumber these funds for fourteen days to permit time for clearance.

In essence, the on-line depositor file contains all the account information associated with ledger cards. This, in turn, has made it possible to establish off-line backup procedures similar to those that existed before timesharing was introduced. If computer service is interrupted, tellers base their transaction postings on trial-balance reports delivered weekly from the computer center to each branch office using the system. With service interrupted, deposits can still be processed routinely, with data reentered from journal items after the system is back on-line. To handle withdrawals in the backup mode, the teller must refer to the printed trial balance. If a withdrawal is processed while service is interrupted, penciled notations are made on the trial-balance report in the controlling branch office.

File protection at the computer center is provided by having two tape units record all transactions processed by each on-line system. The on-line records themselves are stored on CRAM (Card Random Access Memory) files. A considerable amount of processing takes place at the computer center at the close of each on-line day for the savings institutions.

Immediately following the close of the day's business, each teller may interrogate the system to receive closing figures to which he or she must balance. On demand, a supervisor, who enters the system through use of a special key, may call for print-back of transaction details. However, this is usually unnecessary, since each machine creates a detailed journal tape during the day. In addition, a number of reports are prepared on a daily and weekly basis by the data center.

Daily reports include transaction journals for all postings to account, by institution and/or branch. Exception and unusual items are also reported separately. Exceptions occur when an erroneous posting has been made, when a valid account number has no corresponding record on file, or if transactions are authorized by supervisory override. Special situations include the opening of new accounts, large transactions, the closing of accounts, and so on. Trial balances, printed weekly, include full records of all accounts, listed numerically by branch.

Because the date of the last transaction is always in the on-line file, the trial-balance reports have a built-in audit trail. Auditors reviewing a savings institution can track the transaction history of an account simply by referring back to trial balances corresponding with the dates of previous transactions.

Such savings account processing services are provided on a flat-rate basis—currently at a rate of $1 per year per account. Obviously, the volume inherent in this industry has helped to make timesharing financially attractive to all parties. This figure of $1 per year, which was in effect in 1973, is half the amount charged when most timesharing services for savings institutions were introduced in 1965 and 1966.

In mortgage processing, participating institutions are offered a choice of three payment methods that can be used by borrowers: passbooks, statements mailed monthly, or sets of punched-card statement forms mailed annually. All payments are entered at face amounts through the same window machines used for savings. The timesharing program automatically credits payments and indicates whether they are for the amount due, for less than the amount due, or for more than the amount due. Interest payments are figured currently on the basis of principal amounts for loans. The mortgage package includes a capability for status inquiry and the generation of lists of accounts for which payments are overdue.

Since this application and the others described in this chapter are peculiar to certain industries, it is not appropriate to the purposes of this book to discuss them in greater detail, or to describe how the information is used by the managers of the institutions involved. However, any overview of timesharing should recognize that managers whose companies function in regulated or standardized industries have, or probably can expect to have, a relatively high probability of finding—today or in the future—a timesharing system designed to meet their special needs.

6 Documentation Applications (Text Preparation and Editing)

In a world characterized by the increasing availability of, and proliferating requirements for, information of all kinds, the process of *documentation* has become a matter of increasing concern to management. One reason has been the substantial and continuing rise in the cost of clerical and secretarial labor. Authoritative estimates suggest that the cost of producing a "typical" business letter increased more than threefold during the past decade.

At the same time, the quality of business communications—measured in terms of such values as clarity and precision—appears to have declined markedly as increasing numbers of quantitively oriented college graduates have entered into communication-dependent management roles. Lack of proficiency with the written word has become increasingly costly to business management, in terms of both the time it takes to produce documents and the mis-understanding and confusion generated by a lack of clarity. As one result, management processes have become increasingly concerned with editorial revision of correspondence and other written communications generated within a business.

This growing management concern with both the cost and the quality of written communications has focused on two distinct, though related, aspects of business documentation:

1. The need to produce correspondence, reports, and other documents that communicate clearly and effectively.
2. The need to revise documents quickly and inexpensively—in

draft form, to incorporate changes made by the original author and/or other reviewers, or in completed form, to produce revised, updated versions.

TRADITIONAL APPROACHES

Traditional approaches to management's growing documentation problems have centered mainly around the application of stand-alone, repetitive typewriting devices. One of the earliest (and still one of the most common) business applications of such devices was the production of individually typed, "personalized" form letters. Machines operate traditional typewriters to produce a standardized message, stopping to permit the insertion of individualized salutations, variable data, or personalized comments. Various names have been used, over the years, to describe this approach, including "word processing" and "power typing."

The earliest version of such automated typing devices used player piano mechanisms. Piano rolls were punched to activate pneumatic devices that ran a number of typewriters. The piano rolls could be coded so that selected paragraphs or segments of letters could be identified on a selector keyboard.

During the early 1950s, there was a proliferation of automatic typing machines operated by punched paper (and subsequently Mylar) tapes. These devices added a dimension of flexibility, in that the same machine could be used both to prepare a tape and to read it for retyping. Punched-tape units introduced the first practical capability for editorial revision of documents from one version to the next. An operator could use a tape to "play out" a clean copy of a document. When this was edited by a manager, the tape could be replayed and changes incorporated in a new tape, which was punched as a by-product of the playback of the original tape.

During the 1960s, capabilities (and costs) were upgraded still further with the introduction of typewriter units operated by mag-netic-tape devices. Later in the sixties, automatic typing units were introduced that operated from "decks" of loose, magnetically coated cards, adding a dimension of modularity to automatic typing capabilities.

The sixties also saw a proliferation of type*setting* devices, for the composition of text for use in books or other published documents, which could be operated by punched- or magnetic-tape devices.

All of these developments followed a single conceptual pattern: once textual material was captured on reproducible media, it could be carried forward automatically from one version or one document form to the next without the need for clerical repetition. Far from the least of the savings involved was the elimination of the need to proofread—and correct—unchanged portions of the same document. In updating documents, the review-and-correction process could concentrate on areas of change, which are the greatest source of error in typewriting or typesetting (i.e., error correction procedures are themselves more error-prone than straight text capturing).

COMPUTERIZED PROGRAMS

On-line text preparation and editing programs were introduced by the computer industry in the early 1960s. For the first few years, these techniques were used sparingly, largely because direct-access file devices still carried relatively high price tags—and because operating-system software could not yet intermix text editing and other applications effectively. Early applications, therefore, tended to be limited to large, dedicated computer systems owned and operated by individual users (e.g., publishing companies). With the advent of low-cost disk storage devices, however, timesharing-based applications of text preparation and editing expanded rapidly, and a number of timesharing utilities were quick to add such programs to their libraries.

Under these programs, the user operates a timesharing terminal very much as he or she would use a conventional office typewriter. If the typist catches an error as it is committed, the machine can simply be backspaced and a corrected entry keyed in. Texts prepared in this manner can be as short as form letters, as long as full-length books. Printouts can be recalled, under programmed formats, either on user terminals or on high-speed line printers using upper- and lowercase character sets.

Timesharing text preparation and editing programs provide a number of advantages that were not available under the serial processing approach of stand-alone, tape-operated machines:

* The most important advantage of the timesharing approach, as compared with the use of stand-alone devices, is that additions, revisions, or changes to the text can be made at any point without having to rerun the entire text. To change a magnetic-tape text file, for example, the entire text must be rerun at typewriter speed and the machine stopped for revisions or changes. With timesharing text editing, the operator simply codes in the places where information is to be added or deleted, and the computer creates a new text file under program control.

* Once text files have been updated through such simple entries at the user's terminal, the computer can generate new drafts rapidly and inexpensively on high-speed line printers. A line printer producing upper- and lowercase text operates at a speed of 800 to 1000 lines per minute—more than 900 times faster than the highest-capacity stand-alone devices generally available at the beginning of 1973. At this writing, several companies have announced automated typing units that will operate at 30 characters per second, or double the speed of previously available units. Even so, however, a high-speed computer printer is more than 300 times faster than a stand-alone typing unit.

* Timesharing services provide for automatic pagination and formatting—functions that must be manually performed by an operator with stand-alone units. Computerized programs will automatically apply line width and depth formatting to textual material drawn from computer files. The program will also number and identify pages, either at the top or at the bottom. In addition, the program can be instructed to leave designated amounts of blank space at specific points for the insertion of illustrations. These illustration spaces will dovetail automatically with the pagination format established by the computer.

* Computer-generated output media can operate high-speed

typesetting devices automatically. For such applications, the computer can hyphenate words automatically, and can iterate all of the coding necessary to control line width, type size, and type font selection, depending on the capabilities of the individual typesetting machines being utilized. Tape-operated devices also have a capability for producing output media that will operate automatic typesetters. Under many systems, however, it is necessary for the operator to make decisions concerning type specifications, line length, hyphenation, and the like. Interestingly, a number of batch-processing programs available from computer timesharing services accept outputs from tape-operated typewriting units as inputs to typesetting programs. It is becoming increasingly feasible to use off-line typewriting units with tape output as remote batch preparation devices for timesharing text editing and typesetting programs.

- Computer programs also have far greater capabilities for text selection than stand-alone devices. With a computer program, for example, it is possible simply to enter a series of paragraph numbers and have a document, such as a letter or a contract, generated automatically. With a stand-alone typewriting unit, on the other hand, the machine would be idle while the reading device scans a tape to select the desired text segment.

TYPICAL BUSINESS APPLICATIONS

Typical business applications of timesharing text preparation and editing programs are letter writing and the production of major business documents such as manuals, reports, and publications.

Letter Writing

Through the use of either high-speed printers or typewriting terminals, the computer can generate personalized form letters at very high speeds. In some cases it is possible to tailor or individualize form letters on the basis of existing computer file content.

Many charitable organizations, for example, use high-speed printers to generate fund solicitation letters. In one typical application, the computer accepts an input that records a contribution and enters this amount in the body of the letter, extending thanks for the donation. By sensing addresses, the computer program can also select specific paragraphs appealing to contributors in different regions of the country, different states, or different cities.

At a more sophisticated level, a large accounting firm has established a file of appropriate paragraphs that can be used in composing advisory letters to its clients. When staff members of this firm prepare income tax returns for clients, they also generate a working document that includes paragraph numbers. Entry of these numbers generates cover letters to accompany individual tax returns. These letters advise the client of how much is to be paid and what course or courses of action to follow.

Manuals, Reports, and Other Publications

It has been reliably estimated that United States business spends more than $30 billion a year for operational and professional training. A large part of this expenditure is for the production of manuals, reports, and other publications issued in connection with the marketing and utilization of the company's products or services. Because so many business publications are supportive in nature, they must be updated frequently to correspond with product utilization experience, changes in product design, or developments in the business environment.

Increasingly, the content of such documents is being stored in computer files, updated as necessary, and then regenerated quickly. Through the use of computerized text preparation and editing, production cycles for new manuals and project reports are reduced dramatically in comparison with conventional production techniques.

In addition, increasing numbers of timesharing users are able to realize a twofold advantage—improving the appearance of their published end products and also saving money by setting finished documents in type rather than issuing them in typewritten form. The advantages of improved appearance are obvious. A document set in type, with justified lines, is more impressive-looking and neater than one that is typewritten. The typeset product also fits onto far fewer pages. If an instruction manual is issued in double-spaced typewritten format, for example, it will require three to four times as many pages as would be necessary if the same material were typeset in two-column format, also on $8\frac{1}{2}$- by 11-inch paper. In addition, there is a tendency to reproduce typewritten documents on only one side of each sheet of paper; with a typeset document, substantial savings can be realized by using a better-quality paper and printing on both sides. In general, the combined savings in the costs of paper, printing plates, and labor more than offset the additional costs of typesetting (over the costs of typewriting). Still further savings may be realized by storing both the finished documents and the plates for use in subsequent reruns of the publication.

For companies with high volumes of publishing output—professional publishers and news services in particular—additional advantages can be gained from recently introduced techniques for editing and revising text materials through the use of cathode-ray-tube (CRT) terminals. One system of this type was introduced in 1972 by the Associated Press for editing and dispatch control on its national ("A wire") service. News dispatches transmitted by teletypewriter from bureaus throughout the country are entered into the memory of a computer system in New York. Editors receive a continuing listing of the stories in the computer file and their length. These listings are used as "budgets" for work planning and dispatch control. Editors may call up individual stories, page by page, for display on CRT terminals. Changes or insertions can be made through the use of function keys on the terminals and through typing of insertions. When the editing is completed, the story is dispatched over the A wire under automatic computer control. If a more important news story breaks, transmission can be interrupted at the close of the paragraph currently being transmitted. The computer will then pick up the story when line time is available, adding section headings to succeeding "takes" automatically.

In some publishing situations, it is possible to program typesetting devices that will produce finished negatives ready for platemaking for offset printing presses. Specialized suppliers have produced hardware that will ultimately be capable of making up complete newspaper pages under the control of on-line computer terminals. At this writing, implementation of these capabilities is awaiting only the development and debugging of new software.

COST COMPARISONS

The costs of stand-alone typewriting versus timesharing text preparation and editing systems are compared frequently by potential timesharing users. Depending on the circumstances in individual situations, such studies can favor either approach. Factors that bear on the decision to use either the stand-alone or timesharing approach include the following:

- The frequency, extent, and nature of changes made to documents stored on magnetic media will bear on the cost/effectiveness of the system used. Basically, the more frequent or the more complex the change patterns, the more valuable the timesharing approach will be. Conversely, if documents are retyped frequently with relatively few changes, stand-alone systems may have an advantage.
- The productivity expected from the system and the length of the documents typically processed will also be important selection criteria. In general, the longer the document, the more valuable the automatic formatting capabilities of a computer will be. Also, the higher the productivity, the more cost/effective a computer will be. The obvious cost benefit in this area lies in the application of high-speed printers for volume output. In addition, however, with files on timesharing computers it is less expensive to double production by adding a second terminal than by installing a second stand-alone typing unit.
- The availability of a terminal can be a significant factor. If a company already has a suitable computer terminal used for other applications—and if this terminal will be available to meet text preparation requirements—there is an obvious advantage in timesharing. However, if a company is starting from scratch—and if volumes of work or patterns of revision are not controlling factors—it may be more profitable to

install a low-cost stand-alone unit than to acquire a terminal and use a timesharing service.

LOOKING AHEAD

Further growth in the text preparation and editing services offered by timesharing utilities seems particularly imminent in connection with the writing and revising of computer application programs.

The use of computer terminals for program writing under incremental compiling techniques has been discussed briefly in Chapter 3; this technique is also covered in Chapter 10. Under this approach, the programmer interacts with the computer system on an instruction-by-instruction basis. That is, as each programming instruction is entered into a terminal, the computer validates its acceptability for compiling. This practice catches most errors in format or syntax as they are committed. However, the entire program must still be compiled as a unit after all instructions have been entered.

Another approach that is gaining in popularity is to write the coding for an entire program through the use of text preparation techniques. After the program has been completely prepared on a textual basis, an instruction is entered that causes this coded text to be compiled into an operational program in machine language.

The process of entering instructions at a computer terminal is inherently faster and more easily controlled than the traditional technique of writing program coding on paper forms, having the coding keypunched, and then entering it into the computer on a batch basis. Obviously, turnaround is faster. In addition, there is the inherent advantage that the programmer sees what is going into the computer as he writes it, eliminating the potential problem of keypunching errors.

In particular, this technique lends itself well to the writing of programs for business applications in the COBOL language. This is because COBOL uses instructions which are written in English-type format. Since the structuring and syntax of COBOL statements closely resembles that of English sentences, COBOL coding lends itself naturally to text preparation and editing techniques.

In addition, substantially increased power can be derived from on-line programming techniques through the use of file content or text preparation program routines already available in some computer timesharing systems. Program segments already on file within a computer system can be called up and reused for new programs. In writing a COBOL program, for example, the data definition section is highly repeatable from one application to another. Thus a programmer could, in many situations, call up an existing data definition section from a program in file, insert just a few changes, then use the same data definition section in the new program. Three different types or levels of capability can be found as standard features within some on-line programming systems offered by timesharing utilities:

1. Standard coding blocks, or sections, from programs maintained within the timesharing system can be reused. The reuse of the data definition section, cited above, is an example of this application. In addition, existing environment and identification divisions of COBOL programs already on file can be recalled and used again with little or no modification.
2. Tables within text preparation programs can be used for automatic abbreviation or expansion of statements in a COBOL program. For example, if a program is being written to generate an inventory control report, one column might call for a listing of on-hand balances. The programmer could simply enter the initials "OHB." On recognizing these three capitalized letters in combination, the expander routine within the computer program would enter the full name. The programmer would have the working convenience of entering only the abbreviation and still create a well-documented COBOL program.
3. A few timesharing companies have added a special programming feature, logical translators, to the text editing routines used by COBOL programmers. Under these procedures, the programmer simply types his decision table factors in a series of statements entered at the terminal. The computer routine interprets these logical instructions and automatically generates the large volumes of detail coding necessary to apply these logic sequences. At the programmer's discretion, the

original decision table can be left, as a "comment," within the program for better documentation. Thus interpretation and evaluation of program documentation are permanently easier. In addition, the automatic generation of logic table program sequences serves both to save substantial programming time and to speed the transition from source program planning documents to finished coding. Debugging time is also reduced dramatically, because the programmer can verify his logic by reviewing his source documents rather than having to analyze detail coding.

With the discovery of this potential for program writing through text editing techniques, a whole new dimension of market potential has been opened to timesharing companies. With these techniques, timesharing becomes an economically feasible tool for programmers who are developing systems to run on in-house batch computers. The use of timesharing facilities to write programs results in dramatic savings of programming time and money—generally far more than enough to offset the cost of the fees and terminal rentals involved. This potential is enhanced by the ability of many timesharing services to generate COBOL programs in "dialects" needed for compatibility with different computer makes or models. That is, a timesharing computer made by one manufacturer can be programmed to generate coding compatible with the requirements of several other manufacturers.

The text editing approach to program writing is also extremely valuable in the revision of existing programs. For revisions, program codes are called up and treated as though they were straight textual material. New instructions are inserted as needed. Instructions to be changed or deleted are handled in the same way as changes to document texts. When the coding changes have been completed, the program is recompiled by the computer—and revised further as necessary on the basis of diagnostic reports delivered to the programmer.

For either original writing or revisions of programs, an added benefit can be realized by entering test data immediately after a program has been compiled satisfactorily. Thus programs can be debugged and tested before they are entered into and allowed to use time on an in-house computer.

Any astute business manager recognizes that his company's investment in and dependence on documentation can only continue to grow. This applies both to textual documentation and to program coding. In the face of these trends, the evolution of low-cost computer files and timesharing techniques for text processing seems to have happened in the right place at the right time.

7 Management Analysis Applications: An Overview

Management analysis was among the earliest, and continues to be one of the most important, areas for the use of timesharing in business. Applications in this area involve different values and decision criteria for management than the general accounting and record-keeping applications discussed earlier in these pages.

In record-keeping applications the nature of the work involved is highly repetitive. The emphasis in such applications is on a strong commitment and a continuing relationship between the timesharing utility and the user company.

In management analysis applications the picture is quite different. Typically, a management analysis program—for example, a series of financial projections to test alternative budget assumptions—stands by itself. It does not have to be integrated with other programs in a total, overall system.

The significance of this difference in terms of timesharing utilization lies in the nature and purpose of the files that must be maintained on the computer. In accounting and record-keeping applications, integrity of and user control over file content are critical considerations. In management analysis applications, however, files are more nearly akin to electronic scratch pads. They can be used casually to meet special needs, and can almost literally be discarded after they have been used. Operating continuity is not an important consideration in most management analysis applications, so the reliability of files is not as critical as it is in record-keeping applications.

The costs of using timesharing for management analysis applications tend to be of a one-time nature, and the user can generally estimate very early in a project what his final timesharing costs will be. It is the nature of analytical applications that they can be terminated or postponed with relatively little penalty. Continuing fixed costs—a matter of major concern in record-keeping applications—are rarely a consideration in decisions to use timesharing for management analysis applications. The great majority of the costs involved in using timesharing for management analysis are variable. And those few costs that do continue, such as terminal rental and file storage, are comparatively minor.

TYPES OF APPLICATIONS

Management analysis applications of timesharing can be broadly classified as either (1) scientific applications or (2) quantitative management applications.

Scientific applications are associated chiefly with research, design, engineering, architecture, structural analysis, and other activities of a scientific or technical nature. By and large, those who use timesharing for applications of this type are mathematically sophisticated, and such users have naturally become major customers for timesharing utilities. The question of when and how timesharing services are used for such applications is not usually subject to the normal criteria of management decision making, however. Rather, the timesharing service is regarded as a scientific or engineering tool to be used at the discretion of the professionals involved. Thus such applications and their associated decision factors are beyond the scope of this book, which is directed exclusively to the interests of managers.

Quantitative management applications can be further classified as either (1) financial analysis applications or (2) operational analysis applications. Applications of timesharing services for financial analysis are described in Chapters 8 and 9. Such applications include financial projections, depreciation analyses, rate-of-return calculations, accounting method comparisons, and the like. In operational analysis, timesharing is used for management simulation exercises, for scheduling (including PERT and other critical-path techniques), and for related problem-solving activities. Such applications are discussed in Chapter 10.

The user of timesharing services for quantitative management applications is likely to hold a planning, analytical, or purely decision-making position in his company—as distinguished from the operational manager who is more likely to be concerned with record-keeping applications. Such users are found in small companies as well as large. Typical uses of timesharing in a small company are, for example, applications associated with the acquisition of financing or the offering of securities to the public.

Managers in large companies generally share the same motives in using timesharing for management analysis purposes as their counterparts in smaller organizations. In large companies, however, the decision to use timesharing is likely to include consideration of whether a particular application should be handled on the company's own in-house computer or through an outside service organization. Factors that bear on this decision include the need for fast turnaround and the availability of appropriate software and programming languages. These can be important considerations. In many companies computer installations were designed exclusively to handle conventional business data-processing applications and are not well equipped to support mathematically oriented languages or programming efforts. In such companies, management analysis applications are often handled through outside timesharing service organizations, many of which have all of the programs and software needed for analytical applications available on an off-the-shelf basis.

A WORD OF CAUTION

An attitude of caution is particularly important with regard to the structuring of analytical-type applications of timesharing. Among the horror stories of the timesharing industry are many which tell of talent and money wasted by managers who have let themselves get carried away with the capabilities of timesharing services that offer large simulation models and other sophisticated techniques.

There is a real danger that the sophistication and technical fascination of the timesharing tool may become ends in themselves, obscuring the pragmatic business purposes that led the company to use that tool in the first place. Low-yield projects of this type are often initiated by young managers or employees who used timesharing systems in college and for whom sophisticated computer applications are sometimes more intriguing than other aspects of their day-to-day business responsibilities. More than one promising business career has been detoured because a young man or woman with insufficient practical experience was permitted to roam too often down unproductive paths.

This danger, of course, is not unique to timesharing; it exists to some degree in connection with any use of computers for analytical-type applications. Where an in-house system is used, however, normal organizational and operational disciplines tend to minimize opportunities for applications that have not been adequately planned or structured to be pursued beyond the point of no return.

8 Financial Projections

In most companies, financial projections are performed by and for top management and its key advisers. Because of the importance of the decisions involved and the value of the time of the people who make those decisions, the advantages of timesharing are perhaps more readily apparent in financial projection applications than in most other areas of management analysis. As a result, financial projections represent an ideal opportunity for the company's leaders to gain firsthand experience in the use of computers in general, and computer timesharing in particular, as a tool of day-to-day management decision making.

Not all managements, however, perform financial projections for the same reasons, or regard such projections with the same degree of involvement and interest. A great deal depends on the basic stimulus that led management to undertake a financial projection program in the first place. Increasingly such programs are being initiated by an alert member of the top management team itself, or by one of its key advisers, in which case there is generally a good deal of respect and enthusiasm for the use of financial projections as a management tool. There are still many companies, however, including some very large and successful enterprises, in which financial projections are regarded by top management essentially as a defensive exercise—something it got prodded into doing by the company's bankers, stockholders, securities dealers, or those bright young Harvard Business School types in the controller's department.

Whatever the case—whether the financial projection effort is self-initiated and well appreciated by top management or is a defensive, compliance-type program aimed mainly at satisfying someone else—the objective should be to derive the greatest possible benefit from such efforts for the company's future well-being. Valid financial projections help management to allocate scarce resources and to anticipate future earnings. Through analyses of projected resources and earnings, management can determine whether it will be necessary to secure new resources or whether excess resources can be distributed to the company's shareholders. To accomplish this, management must commit itself to an ongoing analysis of the company that is aimed at (1) identifying the factors that affect its financial results and (2) assessing and comparing the effects of likely or possible changes in each of these factors. In short, and at the risk of oversimplification, a financial projection program is a tool through which management undertakes to develop an understanding of the interrelationships and interactions between those areas of the company's operations that are represented by balance sheet items.

Before considering how timesharing can contribute to this process, it might be well first to review the nature of the process and the limitations of manual projection techniques.

STARTING A PROJECTION PROGRAM

To get started with a financial projection program, management must begin with a commitment of its own time and interest. This commitment need not necessarily be of major proportions. As indicated earlier, the type of program will, in effect, make its costs known early in the project cycle. The costs and human factors involved are not, and should not be distorted to be, major.

Rather, management must spend the time necessary to analyze and test the logic of the assumptions that give the company its financial direction. If projections have been prepared manually in the past, for example, a good starting point is to compare last year's projections with the actual, reported results. Such a comparison should help to identify those planning assumptions and other projection inputs that have proved valid, and those that have not.

In shaping a financial projection program, management must also make a basic decision as to how extensive the information developed should be. The choice here lies between limiting the effort to simple income statement and balance sheet projections or undertaking a somewhat more complex program, including cash flow forecasts.

It is important that the individuals making these decisions understand exactly what is involved in the projection program and that they set the parameters for it. A lack of sufficient interest or involvement on the part of top management at this critical stage can lead to a highly sophisticated, mathematically complex financial projection program whose results may not be sufficiently meaningful or useful to management.

A basic management responsibility lies in identifying the logical relationships that exist among the various balance sheet accounts. These determinations by management provide the key factors that will be incorporated in the projection effort.

A financial projection program can follow either of two courses. One approach is to start by establishing objectives for the company's financial performance and then making projections to determine the resources necessary to achieve those objectives under various conditions. The second, quite opposite, approach is to begin by identifying the resources available and use the projection process to determine what results can be anticipated as a return from these resources under various assumptions.

Traditionally there has been a tendency to follow the second course—to use existing resources as the prime input to a financial projection system, developing data for results available with these resources. It can be argued, however, that the first approach is more consistent with modern management thinking, which holds that all planning should begin with the setting of objectives. Under this approach, projection techniques are aimed primarily at determining what resources are necessary to accomplish the desired objectives. If those resources are not obtainable, the projection process is repeated with different sets of objectives and resources until an acceptable balance is attained.

Either of these approaches can be used effectively. Which one a particular management chooses to follow will reflect that management's individual philosophy and style.

Once management has determined the basic approach to be followed, the next step is to identify the information results to be delivered by the financial projection system. This identification of results is associated closely with the development of preliminary specifications for processing logic. The processing specifications, in turn, help establish an understanding of other system requirements, including data file content, file sizes, computer capacity requirements, software needs, and programming languages.

At this point it can be determined whether a computer will be necessary to perform the projections and, if so, what kind of computer should be used. Because of the large volumes of data to be processed and the complexity of the interrelationships between the various elements involved in financial projections for most companies today, the computer will generally be recognized as an efficient way to get the job done quickly. Whether this determination entails a formal cost-justification study will vary according to the company's previous experience with computers and, again, its individual management style.

If it is decided to do the projection modeling on a computer, the next question, obviously, is "Which computer?" In general, the choice will be between the company's own computer, a batch-processing service bureau capable of providing next-day turnaround, or an interactive timesharing system provided by a utility. Which of these alternatives management chooses will reflect a number of considerations, including management's sense of urgency about getting the work done quickly, the value of interactive turnaround to the individuals who will perform the financial projections, the level of management participating, the availability of time on the company's computer, and comparative costs.

If it is decided to handle the financial projection program through timesharing, the course of action can be expected to follow more or less along the lines of the case history described in the remaining sections of this chapter.

A TYPICAL PROBLEM

ABC Food Products operates a chain of 25 restaurants located in four states. The business has grown rapidly in the ten years since ABC was founded. Operations are profitable, and an aggressive, competent management is involved in both running and owning the business. Established cash flow patterns, supplemented by bank financing of property, buildings, and equipment, are adequate to sustain a projected growth rate of 20 percent a year.

ABC Food Products and its owners have matured to a point where long-range consideration is being given to the sale of a substantial portion of the company's closely held stock, either to a larger company or to the public. To meet this objective, ABC's management wants to be able to predict, with reasonable accuracy, the steps necessary to maintain the company's projected growth rate.

Existing data that will serve as a basis for financial projections indicate that the company operates six basically different types of restaurants. Within each of these categories, sales, construction costs, and operating costs have remained fairly constant, regardless of geographic location. However, revenues and costs do vary substantially according to type of restaurant. Throughout its brief ten-year history, ABC has, quite naturally, experimented continually with the introduction of new types of restaurants. As each new idea has been put into practice, supporting revenue and cost projections have been prepared.

In the past, the company has used a limited form of financial projection. At the end of each fiscal year, the controller has spent about a week updating a four-year projection of income statements, balance sheets, and cash flow forecasts. One of the limitations of this planning exercise, however, has been the fact that the controller has had to do most of the work himself because of the confidentiality of much of the data. Because the controller has not had enough personal time to devote to this activity, the resulting financial projections have been neither as frequent nor as reliable as ABC's management would have liked. The controller's procedures have been quite informal. He has contacted middle managers to gather data on plans for new restaurants, changes in financing arrangements, anticipated wage rates, and the like. This information has then been summarized on a succession of worksheets, ultimately leading to balances on the four-year projections.

Under this manual approach, for example, a sales forecast was made for each new restaurant to be opened during the projected four-year period, using a constant factor for each type of restaurant. However, new restaurant openings are highly dependent on construction schedules, availability of financing, local labor negotiations, and a number of other notoriously unpredictable factors—changes in any of which can (and, in ABC's case, often did) cause significant delays in planned restaurant openings. With the controller's manual forecasting techniques it was impossible to update financial projections on a current basis—or even to run a series of projections based on varying assumptions about construction completion during the annual forecasting cycle.

HOW TIMESHARING CAN HELP

The use of timesharing seemed especially well suited both to the objectives of ABC's management and to the nature of its financial projection needs.

One condition favoring the use of timesharing was that ABC's financial projections involved the repetition of whole sets of calculations a number of times, with only minor changes in their basic format to accommodate varying assumptions to be tested by management. For example, corporate sales were always determined by multiplying the number of open restaurants of each type by the projected annual sales volume for that type of restaurant. Similar approaches could be used in determining the great majority of the account balances involved in the projections.

A second factor favoring the use of timesharing was the need for rapid turnaround to accommodate the busy schedules of the controller and ABC's other top managers. Through the use of timesharing, management could interact with the computer on an instantaneous-response basis in describing hypothetical conditions and deriving forecasts of their consequences.

Having decided to explore timesharing, ABC's management authorized a four-stage analysis of costs, other requirements, and benefits. The steps followed in this analysis were:

1. Preliminary design of report formats.

2. Establishment of general system design characteristics.
3. Estimation of development and operating costs.
4. Comparison of these costs with the benefits to be obtained.

Report Formats

Formats for the presentation of financial projection data were tailored to the specific objectives and needs of ABC's management. One of the primary considerations in this regard was management's decision that the reports should be designed and used strictly for internal management purposes, rather than as a vehicle for presentation to banks or other sources of financing.

Since financial projections had previously been prepared in ABC, it seemed desirable to continue to prepare the same basic kinds of reports—income statements, balance sheets, and cash flow projections—when timesharing was introduced, to assure maximum continuity and comparability. For the same reasons it was also decided to continue, at least in the beginning, to produce

ABC FOOD PRODUCTS, INC.

SUMMARY INCOME STATEMENTS

000 OMITTED

	1968	1969	1970	1971	1972
SALES	278431	321731	417831	506231	558131
COST OF SALES	196560	228448	299033	364919	403987
RENT	14196	16361	21166	25586	28181
DEPRECIATION EXPENSE	8799	8974	9272	9562	9739
GENERAL AND ADM EXPENSE	26838	27078	27352	27650	27942
INTEREST EXPENSE	1596	1355	823	406	208
PROFIT SHARING EXPENSE	1000	1000	1000	1000	1000
TOTAL COSTS AND EXPENSES	248989	283216	358646	429123	471056
INCOME BEFORE TAXES	29442	38515	59185	77108	87075
TAX EXPENSE	13923	20085	30988	40441	45697
INCOME AFTER TAXES	15519	18431	28197	36667	41378

Figure 8.1 Income statement—ABC Foods.

ABC FOOD PRODUCTS, INC.

SUMMARY BALANCE SHEETS

OOO OMITTED

	1968	1969	1970	1971	1972
-----ASSETS------					
CASH	41811	60173	98103	136843	182388
ACCOUNTS RECEIVABLE	4074	4084	4094	4104	4114
INVENTORY	5922	5959	6047	6101	6101
PREPAID EXPENSES	2205	2215	2225	2235	2245
CURRENT ASSETS	54012	72431	110469	149283	194848
BUILDING AND EQUIPMENT	76482	77332	79717	81307	81947
TRANSPORTATION EQUIPMENT	5586	5518	5526	5534	5542
IMPROVEMENTS	14490	15219	15219	15219	15219
CONSTRUCTION IN PROGRESS	0	450	50	225	600
ACCUMULATED DEPRECIATION	- 36771	- 45745	- 55017	- 64579	- 74318
OTHER ASSETS	8043	8076	8169	8229	8253
TOTAL ASSETS	121842	133281	164133	195218	232092
-----LIABILITIES-----					
ACCOUNTS PAYABLE	12642	13900	16340	17876	18452
TAXES PAYABLE	7161	6242	10983	9533	5336
ACCRUED LIABILITIES	7098	7108	7118	7128	7138
PROFIT SHARING PAYABLE	5460	5484	5508	.5532	5556
LONG TERM DEBT - CURRENT	8862	5993	6589	1244	1044
CURRENT LIABILITIES	41223	38726	46538	41313	37526
LONG TERM DEBT	12516	8021	2863	2507	1790
TOTAL LIABILITIES	53739	46747	49401	43820	39316
-----STOCKHOLDERS EQUITY-----					
COMMON STOCK	19341	19341	19341	19341	19341
RETAINED EARNINGS	48762	67193	95390	132057	173435
TOTAL EQUITY	68103	86534	114731	151398	192776
LIABILITIES AND EQUITY	121842	133281	164133	195218	232092

Figure 8.2   Balance sheet—ABC Foods.

four-year projections on an annual basis in the same degree of detail as the projections previously prepared for ABC's controller.

All of these decisions were based on the assumption that, initially, ABC's management would use the projection data in much the same way that it had used the data previously prepared by the controller. At the same time, however, it was recognized that, as management gained more experience with the preparation and use of more timely and accurate financial projections, and with

ABC FOOD PRODUCTS, INC.

CASH FLOW REPORT

000 OMITTED

	1969	1970	1971	1972
-----SOURCES OF CASH-----				
INCOME	13431	28197	36667	41378
DEPRECIATION	8974	9272	9562	9739
TRANSPORTATION EQUIPMENT DECR	68	0	0	0
CONSTRUCTION IN PROCESS DECR	0	400	0	0
ACCOUNTS PAYABLE INCR	1258	2440	1536	576
TAXES PAYABLE INCR	0	4742	0	0
ACCRUED LIABILITIES INCR	10	10	10	10
PROFIT SHARING PAYABLE INCR	24	24	24	24
LONG TERM DEBT - CURRENT INCR	0	596	0	0
TOTAL SOURCES	28765	45681	47799	51726
-----USES OF CASH-----				
ACCOUNTS RECEIVABLE DECR	10	10	10	10
INVENTORY DECR	37	88	54	0
PREPAID EXPENSES DECR	10	10	10	10
BUILDING AND EQUIPMENT DECR	850	2385	1590	640
TRANSPORTATION EQUIPMENT DECR	0	8	8	8
IMPROVEMENTS DECR	729	0	0	0
CONSTRUCTION IN PROGRESS DECR	450	0	175	375
OTHER ASSETS DECR	33	93	60	24
TAXES PAYABLE INCR	919	0	1450	4197
LONG TERM DEBT - CURRENT INCR	2870	0	5344	200
LONG TERM DEBT INCR	4495	5158	356	717
TOTAL USES	10403	7752	9058	6181
CASH INCREASE	18362	37930	38741	45545

Figure 8.3   Cash flow projection—ABC Foods.

the interactive timesharing mode, changes in the frequency, format, and content of reports could, and probably would, be made to serve other management purposes.

The formats of ABC's three basic reports, as prepared through timesharing, are shown in Figure 8.1 (income statement), Figure 8.2 (balance sheet), and Figure 8.3 (cash flow projection).

System Design

Having determined what reports would be produced and what their formats would be, the next step was to determine the content and layout of the files from which the reports would be developed and what processing would be necessary to develop those files.

Particular attention was paid to the development of techniques and specifications for input to the system. In this case, since the controller did have previous experience with the use of timesharing, it was possible to design a system for maximum efficiency, sacrificing some ease of input operations.

The input format adopted for ABC Food Products is illustrated in Figure 8.4. By entering 40 lines of data using eight tabular positions per line, it is possible to generate a complete set of financial forecast reports for ABC Food Products.

Note that the line-by-line entries called for as input correspond with coded numbers on the chart of balance sheet and profit and loss statement accounts developed for ABC, as shown in Figure 8.5.

In considering the correlation of the input format with the chart of accounts, note that spaces are provided in lines 1–5 for beginning balances in each of the 34 accounts. Then spaces are provided to enter forecasted figures in each of the 34 accounts for 16 quarters into the future. (As noted earlier, ABC elected to use its current, audited year plus four future years as its financial forecasting cycle.)

Examples of the processing logic to be performed on these input data are the descriptions of equations for balance sheet and profit and loss factors shown in Figure 8.6.

Because turnaround time was an important consideration in

The Input file is named / DATA / and has the following format:

Line 1	Beginning balance, account 0-7	—	—	—	—	—	—	—	—
Line 2	Beginning balance, account 8-15	—	—	—	—	—	—	—	—
Line 3	Beginning balance, account 16-23	—	—	—	—	—	—	—	—
Line 4	Beginning balance, account 24-31	—	—	—	—	—	—	—	—
Line 5	Beginning balance, account 32-34	—	—	—					
Line 6	Quarterly dollar change in Accounts Receivable	—							
Line 7	Quarterly dollar change in Prepaid Expenses	—							
Line 8	Quarterly dollar change in Accrued Liabilities	—							
Line 9	Change in General & Administrative Expenses, Quarter 1-8	—	—	—	—	—	—	—	—
Line 10	Change in General & Administrative Expenses, Quarter 9-16	—	—	—	—	—	—	—	—
Line 11	Change in Transportation Equipment, Quarter 1-8	—	—	—	—	—	—	—	—
Line 12	Change in Transportation Equipment, Quarter 9-16	—	—	—	—	—	—	—	—
Line 13	Change in Profit Sharing Expense, Quarter 1-8	—	—	—	—	—	—	—	—
Line 14	Change in Profit Sharing Expense, Quarter 9-16	—	—	—	—	—	—	—	—
Line 15	Change in Cost of Sales, Quarter 1-8	—	—	—	—	—	—	—	—
Line 16	Change in Cost of Sales, Quarter 9-16	—	—	—	—	—	—	—	—
Line 17	Change in Construction in Progress, Quarter 1-8	—	—	—	—	—	—	—	—
Line 18	Change in Construction in Progress, Quarter 9-16	—	—	—	—	—	—	—	—
Line 19	Change in Profit Sharing Payable, Quarter 1-8	—	—	—	—	—	—	—	—
Line 20	Change in Profit Sharing Payable, Quarter 9-16	—	—	—	—	—	—	—	—
Line 21	By shop type 1-8, Quarterly Sales	—	—	—	—	—	—	—	—
Line 22	By shop type 1-8, Inventory	—	—	—	—	—	—	—	—
Line 23	By shop type 1-8, Restaurant Equipment	—	—	—	—	—	—	—	—
Line 24	By shop type 1-8, Other Assets	—	—	—	—	—	—	—	—
Line 25	By shop type 1-8, Cost as Percent of Sales	—	—	—	—	—	—	—	—
Line 26	By shop type 1-8, Shop openings, Quarter 1 — Prior Year	—	—	—	—	—	—	—	—
Line 27	By shop type 1-8, Shop openings, Quarter 2 — Prior Year	—	—	—	—	—	—	—	—
Line 28	By shop type 1-8, Shop openings, Quarter 3 — Prior Year	—	—	—	—	—	—	—	—
Line 29	By shop type 1-8, Shop openings, Quarter 4 — Prior Year	—	—	—	—	—	—	—	—
Line 30	By shop type 1-8, Shop openings, Quarter 1	—	—	—	—	—	—	—	—
Line 31	By shop type 1-8, Shop openings, Quarter 2	—	—	—	—	—	—	—	—
Line 32	By shop type 1-8, Shop openings, Quarter 3	—	—	—	—	—	—	—	—
Line 33	By shop type 1-8, Shop openings, Quarter 4	—	—	—	—	—	—	—	—
Line 34	By shop type 1-8, Shop openings, Quarter 5	—	—	—	—	—	—	—	—
Line 35	By shop type 1-8, Shop openings, Quarter 6	—	—	—	—	—	—	—	—
Line 36	By shop type 1-8, Shop openings, Quarter 7	—	—	—	—	—	—	—	—
Line 37	By shop type 1-8, Shop openings, Quarter 8	—	—	—	—	—	—	—	—
Line 38	By shop type 1-8, Shop openings, Quarter 9	—	—	—	—	—	—	—	—
Line 39	By shop type 1-8, Shop openings, Quarter 10	—	—	—	—	—	—	—	—
Line 40	By shop type 1-8, Shop openings, Quarter 11	—	—	—	—	—	—	—	—

Figure 8.4   Input format—ABC Foods.

ABC FOOD PRODUCTS
FINANCIAL PROJECTION SYSTEM
CHART OF ACCOUNTS

Account Number	Account Title
0	Sales
1	Cost of Sales
2	Rent
3	Depreciation Expense
4	General and Admin. Expense
5	Interest Expense
6	Profit Sharing Expense
7	Total Costs and Expenses
8	Income Before Taxes
9	Tax Expense
10	Income After Taxes
11	Cash
12	Accounts Receivable
13	Inventory
14	Prepaid Expenses
15	Current Assets
16	Buildings and Equipment
17	Transportation Equipment
18	Improvements
19	Construction in Process
20	Accumulated Depreciation
21	Other Assets
22	Total Assets
23	Accounts Payable
24	Taxes Payable
25	Accrued Liabilities
26	Profit Sharing Payable
27	Long Term Debt—Current
28	Current Liabilities
29	Long Term Debt
30	Total Liabilities
31	Common Stock
32	Retained Earnings
33	Total Equity
34	Liabilities and Equity

Figure 8.5   Chart of accounts—ABC Foods.

ABC's decision to use timesharing, it was decided to have all reports printed out directly on the company's terminal.

At the time this general system design was undertaken, the company's commitment and cost exposure were still nominal.

Cost Estimates

As the system design was being completed, a study was made to determine the likely development and operating costs. A major purpose of this study was, obviously, to permit management to compare the potential costs with the potential benefits to be derived from the results of the financial projection effort.

The following cost factors were included in the study:

- Costs of developing the input parameters or variables that would be used by the computer model to prepare the projections.
- Costs of storing the data files.
- Costs of storing the processing program itself.
- Charges for computer processing.

ABC FOOD PRODUCTS
FINANCIAL PROJECTION SYSTEM
CALCULATION OF INCOME STATEMENT BALANCES

The account balances for this program are calculated as follows:

Sales

Quarterly balances are one-fourth of the base year balance plus (1) an increase to account for a full year's sale at shops opened in the base year, and (2) the sales at new shops. All openings in a quarter are considered to have been on the first day of that quarter. Up to eight shop types may be handled.

Cost of Sales

Quarterly balances are one-fourth of the base year balance, plus a percentage of sales changes by type, minus changes in rent and depreciation expense. Changes may also be directly input for each quarter.

Rent

Quarterly balances are one-quarter of the base year balance plus a percentage of sales changes. The percentage is input for each year.

Depreciation Expense

Quarterly balances are a percentage of the ending balance in each fixed asset account. Separate rates are used for each of the fixed asset accounts.

General and Administrative Expense

Quarterly balances are one-fourth of the base year balance plus changes input for each quarter.

Figure 8.6   Calculation of income statement balances—ABC Foods.

- Terminal and communication link costs.
- Costs represented by the time of the terminal operator.

The key cost elements associated with developing the system for ABC Foods are shown in Figure 8.7. It should be noted that ABC's management decided to have the design and programming work done by an outside vendor, since the company had no data-processing capability of its own.

Cost/Benefit Comparison

The completed cost estimates were used to determine whether the timesharing approach could be cost-justified for ABC's financial projection application.

In this case the cost/benefit comparison was based on an assumption that eight sets of projections would be prepared annually—two per quarter. The timesharing costs shown in Figure 8.7 were compared with estimates for the old manual procedures of 20 hours for the preparation of each projection at a cost of $15 per hour (reflecting the fact that the work was being done by the controller). On this basis, it was determined that reduced operat-

ABC FOOD PRODUCTS
FINANCIAL PROJECTION SYSTEM
SYSTEM COST ESTIMATES

Element	Volume	Cost
Input	200-400 parameters	$5-10 per projection
Storage	13,000 characters	$13 per month
Processing		$5-15 per projection
Output	50 minutes	$15 per projection
Design and Programming	3-5 weeks	$3,000-5,000 one time cost
System Operation	5 hours	$100 per projection

Figure 8.7 Timesharing system costs—ABC Foods.

ing costs, once the timesharing system was operational, would pay for the startup expenses in less than two years.

The cost comparison projections used by ABC Food Products are illustrated in Figure 8.8.

Once ABC's management decided to use timesharing, the next step, obviously, was to select a vendor to provide the timesharing services. The processes followed and the decision criteria applied were similar to those discussed in Chapter 11 of this book.

A HAPPY ENDING

ABC Food Products was acquired by one of the larger companies in its field about two years after the timesharing-based financial projection program was implemented. Data developed through the use of the financial projection model played a major role in the negotiations that led to the merger.

This type of happy ending does not, of course, follow automatically from the use of timesharing. Neither is it a prerequisite

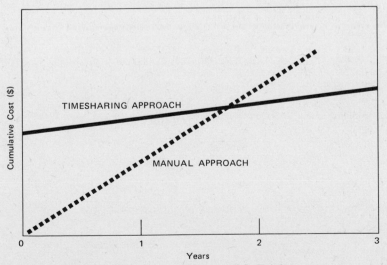

Figure 8.8 Cost comparison projections—ABC Foods.

to the successful use of a financial projection system. In the case described, for example, the system would have been just as valuable if ABC's forecasts had shown that the company's available resources could not support its projected expansion plans. Financial forecasting through timesharing is, basically, a tool to help management ponder its future with improved reliability. Managers contemplating an application of this kind should not succumb to overoptimism or allow themselves to be oversold on the benefits of the system. The value of any financial projection effort increases in direct proportion to the realism of management's perspective.

9 Financial Analysis

Financial managers can frequently make profitable use of time-sharing services, for various analytical purposes, in a manner similar to the financial projection procedures described in the preceding chapter. Financial analysis applications, too, tend to be characterized by low volumes of data and one-time (or infrequent) utilization.

There is, however, an important difference between financial projections and other types of financial analysis as far as the use of timesharing is concerned. Many financial analysis applications have evolved to a point where libraries of standard programs are available from timesharing utilities, and this has encouraged a more widespread use of timesharing as a financial analysis tool. There is also, of course, an almost infinite potential for the development and use of unique, special-purpose financial analysis programs within individual companies.

In this chapter we consider the use of computer timesharing to perform six common types of financial analysis:

1. Depreciation and amortization studies.
2. Interest calculations.
3. Capital budgeting.
4. Studies of the effects of contemplated changes in reporting methods.
5. Tax computations.
6. Investment analysis (including lease-or-buy and acquisition decisions).

DEPRECIATION AND AMORTIZATION STUDIES

The preparation of depreciation schedules was one of the earliest application areas for which timesharing utilities developed and offered standardized programs on a "library" basis. The resulting reduction in user preparation costs and data storage costs led to increased use of timesharing for such applications. This last point is significant in understanding the development of the timesharing industry. There are obviously greater incentives for using timesharing when a program with broad general applicability is available as part of the timesharing utility's basic service charge. To the extent that a particular company can use that standardized program, its application preparation costs will be reduced dramatically. In addition, the company will eliminate or substantially reduce the not insignificant cost of maintaining its own proprietary program in semipermanent storage.

Typically, the financial management of a company that has made one or a series of major capital investments will project depreciation and amortization schedules on the basis of a number of alternative approaches. Comparison of the results of such projections helps to determine which of the various permissible methods will be most advantageous to the company. Where new capital investments are involved, it is also possible to compare the effects of treating various items individually, for depreciation purposes, or as parts of groups of assets.

Several timesharing utilities offer program packages that make it possible to prepare depreciation and amortization schedules in a matter of minutes, with very simple input requirements. With one such program, the user indicates:

- The amount of the capital investment.
- Its salvage value.
- Its depreciable (useful) life in years.
- The number of months of depreciation in the first year.
- The types of depreciation schedules to be printed out.

Depreciation methods available in this particular program package include straight-line, declining-balance using varying percentages, declining-balance shifting to straight-line, and sum-of-the-years-digits.

To illustrate the capabilities of such timesharing programs, Figure 9.1 shows a depreciation schedule produced on a user terminal. This particular schedule is for depreciation on a double-declining-balance basis for a capital investment valued at $125,000.

```
TYPE ORIGINAL COST OF THE ASSET....     ? 125000
TYPE ESTIMATED SALVAGE VALUE OF THE ASSET....     ? 12500
TYPE ESTIMATED USEFUL LIFE, IN YEARS....  ? 12
TYPE NUMBER OF MONTHS DEPRECIATION IN THE FIRST YEAR....     ? 8
```

YEAR	DEPRECIATION	TOTAL DEPREC.	BOOK VALUE
1	13888.89	13888.89	111111.11
2	18518.52	32407.41	92592.59
3	15432.10	47839.51	77160.49
4	12860.08	60699.59	64300.41
5	10716.74	71416.32	53583.68
6	8930.61	80346.94	44653.06
7	7442.18	87789.11	37210.89
8	6201.81	93990.93	31009.07
9	5168.18	99159.11	25840.89
10	4306.82	103465.92	21534.08
11	3589.01	107054.94	17945.06
12	2990.84	110045.78	14954.22
13	934.64	110980.42	14019.58

Figure 9.1   Depreciation schedule.

The item has a useful life of 12 years and a scrap value of $12,500. Thus the figures for year 13 on the schedule in Figure 9.1 are the concluding depreciated total and book values for the purchase. Obviously, real-life depreciation and amortization studies could be far more useful if the effects of a wide range of depreciation methods could be projected and compared. To give some idea of the costs involved, a schedule such as that shown in Figure 9.1 can be produced through timesharing for $2 to $3 of computation and terminal connect time.

INTEREST CALCULATIONS

Interest calculations performed through timesharing are used for a wide variety of business purposes. Here again, usage has grown under the stimulus of readily available standardized programs.

Users of interest calculation services offered by timesharing utilities include both borrowing companies and lending institutions. Sophisticated borrowers are, increasingly, performing detailed interest calculations before committing to purchases, particularly where real property is involved. This type of calculation makes it possible to establish a thorough, quantitative understanding of the implications of borrowing—in place of approximations or "seat-of-the-pants" guesstimates. With timesharing, reliable figures can be developed in about the same amount of time that it takes to develop approximations, and for a comparable cost.

For many lending institutions and mortgage bankers the interest calculation programs offered by timesharing utilities have become a standard working tool. With such a program, payment schedules can be developed in the presence of the prospective borrower in a matter of minutes. It is even possible, at insignificant cost, to develop alternative schedules, reflecting a choice of payment programs, as part of the negotiation for the closing of a loan.

Interest calculations are performed through timesharing on the basis of four loan characteristics:

• Principal.
• Monthly or quarterly payment amount.
• Number of months or quarters (term of payment).
• Interest rate.

At least three of these four characteristics must be input to a timesharing program by the user. Given any three parameters of a loan, the computer will provide the fourth. In addition, most timesharing programs can accommodate variables in loan payments (e.g., balloon payments) and/or variable interest rates. Programs developed specifically for lending institutions also have a capability for applying "the rule of 78s" for calculating prepaid interest amortization.

An example of a loan repayment schedule developed through timesharing in a few minutes of terminal time is shown in Figure 9.2.

CAPITAL BUDGETING

Management's job of analyzing alternative investment opportunities and evaluating the consequences of alternative investment decisions can also be aided by the use of timesharing. Again, a number of standardized program packages are available for this purpose.

In effect, capital budgeting is an investment technique based on consideration of the "time value" of money. The premise is that

```
DO YOU WANT AN AMORTIZATION SCHEDULE FOR A
LOAN WITH A BALLOON PAYMENT (Y OR N)? N
GIVEN ANY THREE OF THE FOLLOWING,
THIS PROGRAM WILL COMPUTE THE FOURTH.
    1. PRINCIPAL AMOUNT
    2. MONTHLY PAYMENT (INCLUDING INTEREST)
    3. INTEREST RATE
    4. TERM IN MONTHS
ENTER THE NUMBER OF THE UNKNOWN VARIABLE? 3

ENTER PRINCIPAL AMOUNT OF LOAN? 2444
ENTER AMOUNT OF MONTHLY PAYMENT? 80.4-14
ENTER TERM OF LOAN IN MONTHS? 36
INTEREST RATE IS  11.11 PERCENT

DO YOU WANT AN AMORTIZATION
SCHEDULE FOR THIS LOAN (Y OR N)? Y
ENTER MONTH NUMBER OF 1ST PAYMENT (I.E. SEPTEMBER = 9)   ? 4
DO YOU WANT ANNUAL TOTALS ONLY ( Y OR N )    ? N
```

BEGINNING BALANCE	PAYMENTS PRINCIPAL	INTEREST	ENDING BALANCE
2444.00	57.51	22.63	2386.49
2386.49	58.05	22.09	2328.44
2328.44	58.58	21.56	2269.86
2269.86	59.13	21.01	2210.73
2210.73	59.67	20.47	2151.06
2151.06	60.23	19.91	2090.83
2090.83	60.78	19.36	2030.05
2030.05	61.35	18.79	1968.70
1968.70	61.91	18.23	1906.79
YEAR TOTALS	537.21	184.05	
1906.79	62.49	17.65	1844.30
1844.30	63.07	17.07	1781.24
1781.24	63.65	16.49	1717.59
1717.59	64.24	15.90	1653.35
1653.35	64.83	15.31	1588.52
1588.52	65.43	14.71	1523.08
1523.08	66.04	14.10	1457.04
1457.04	66.65	13.49	1390.39
1390.39	67.27	12.87	1323.13
1323.13	67.89	12.25	1255.24
1255.24	68.52	11.62	1186.72
1186.72	69.15	10.99	1117.56
YEAR TOTALS	789.23	172.45	
1117.56	69.79	10.35	1047.77
1047.77	70.44	9.70	977.33
977.33	71.09	9.05	906.24
906.24	71.75	8.39	834.49
834.49	72.41	7.73	762.07
762.07	73.08	7.06	688.99
688.99	73.76	6.38	615.23
615.23	74.44	5.70	540.78
540.78	75.13	5.01	465.65
465.65	75.83	4.31	389.82
389.82	76.53	3.61	313.29
313.29	77.24	2.90	236.05
YEAR TOTALS	881.51	80.17	
236.05	77.95	2.19	158.10
158.10	78.68	1.46	79.42
79.42	79.40	.74	.01
.01	.01	.00	.00
YEAR TOTALS	236.05	4.38	
GRAND TOTALS	2444.00	441.05	

Figure 9.2   Loan repayment schedule.

a dollar which is available and invested today is worth more than a dollar which is available and invested in some future year. This greater worth of today's dollar is based primarily on the interim earning power derived from investing now and realizing predictable yields in the immediate, intermediate, or long-term future. Consideration of the effects of anticipated inflation or devaluation may be included in such analyses, but the *earning power of invested funds* is the primary consideration in capital budgeting exercises.

Packaged timesharing programs available to support such analyses provide for application, at the user's choice, of either rate-of-return analysis or discounted-cash-flow methods of evaluating alternative investment opportunities. Depending on the option selected, the terminal printout may be in terms of yield, present value, or both. Figures represent positive cash flows (receipts) or negative cash flows (payments).

Information that the user must input can be limited to cash outlays, cash returns, and timing of the investment, if the output is to consist of yield data only. If present value is to be calculated, the discount rate must also be entered.

One of the most important advantages of using timesharing for capital budgeting is its fast turnaround capability. Top management usually participates in the capital budgeting process, because only top management can make many of the assumptions and provide many of the values involved. (For example, the input for cash return on an investment is based chiefly on assumptions that top management must make, in the light of past experience and future expectations. The same applies to discount rates for the determination of present values.) Such top management participation, of course, places a premium on responsiveness.

Figure 9.3 shows a computer printout of a capital budgeting forecast for an investment of $67,000 which will realize an annual cash flow of $10,000 for ten succeeding years. The printout includes both the interactive conversation representing the input of these parameters to the computer program and the results of the computation. These results include a projection table prepared by the computer.

At the top of the printout, note that the user has asked that both yield and present value be calculated. The user then enters

RUN

INSTRUCTIONS?   1=YES   0=NO(ASSUMES DATA IS ENTERED)? 0

ENTER MODE OF OPERATION (1=DISCOUNT TO ZERO; 2=PRESENT VALUE)? 1

THE DISCOUNTED RATE OF RETURN IS   8.03 PERCENT.

ANALYSIS OF CASH FLOWS AND DISCOUNTED VALUES:

YEAR	ANNUAL CASH FLOW	CUMULATIVE CASH FLOW	PRESENT VALUE	CUMULATIVE VALUE
1	-67000.00	-67000.00	-67000.00	-67000.00
2	10000.00	-57000.00	9256.40	-57743.60
3	10000.00	-47000.00	8568.10	-49175.50
4	10000.00	-37000.00	7930.98	-41244.53
5	10000.00	-27000.00	7341.23	-33903.29
6	10000.00	-17000.00	6795.34	-27107.95
7	10000.00	-7000.00	6290.05	-20817.90
8	10000.00	3000.00	5822.32	-14995.59
9	10000.00	13000.00	5389.37	-9606.21
10	10000.00	23000.00	4988.62	-4617.59
11	10000.00	33000.00	4617.67	0.08

Figure 9.3   Capital budgeting forecast.

the amount of the investment as a negative value and the projected cash flows for each year as positive amounts. In the computer printout, minus signs appear before figures indicating the status of the investment until the point at which full recovery is realized.

Based on the user's input, the computer calculates a rate of return of 8.03 percent for the investment.

In the tabular projection, the computer prints out the following data:

- *Column 1* lists the years analyzed.
- *Column 2* lists the cash flow for each of the 11 years, beginning with the investment of $67,000 as a negative amount and showing the $10,000 of cash flow in each succeeding year as a positive amount.
- *Column 3* shows cumulative cash flow. The figures indicate the net cash inflow or outflow position of the investment up

to the indicated year. In this projection, payback is realized during the eighth year.

- *Column 4* lists the present value of the investment, year-by-year, on a discounted basis. Thus, where column 2 shows a cash flow of $10,000 for the second year, column 4 discounts this amount to $9256.40. As in column 2, cash flow values are positive numbers.

- *Column 5* shows cumulative return on the investment based on discounted values for each year's cash receipts.

It was in calculating the figures in column 5 that the computer derived the rate of return of 8.03 percent. The instructions that the capital budgeting forecast be carried for ten years into the future, with a net cash flow of $10,000 annually, established the parameters. The computer then calculated discounted-cash-flow values to zero over the stipulated period. As shown in column 5, payback is realized during the last year.

Note that the final figure in column 5 shows a positive value of 8 cents. This is a rounding error made by the computer, and it is obviously immaterial in this situation. Rounding errors of this type are frequently encountered in financial analyses performed by computers.

CHANGES IN REPORTING METHODS

When changes in reporting methods are being contemplated by management, the impact of such changes can be analyzed and compared with the help of timesharing. In effect, a timesharing program makes it possible to project the appearance and content of the company's financial statements under its present methods of reporting and any alternative method or methods that may be under consideration.

A typical situation in which such projections might be used is that of a company with material inventory amounts that is contemplating a change to the LIFO (last in, first out) method of inventory valuation. A program could be written, for use in a timesharing system, to calculate the impact of the change in inventory valuation method upon both the company's financial statements and its tax returns. In considering whether to change to the LIFO method in a period of rising prices, for example, management would weigh the decrease in assets in the financial statements against the lower tax costs resulting from the change in reporting methods. Since such a change in reporting methods is not readily reversed, it is important that management consider the consequences and financial impact of its decision thoroughly. The use of a timesharing system, as described, is one way to provide definitive data on which to base such a decision.

A timesharing system can also serve as a working tool for the development of adjustments to financial statements. This can be illustrated best, perhaps, by a highly simplified example.

Suppose that a company has a long-established policy of selling its products to selected customers on extended terms without interest. Generally accepted accounting principles require that these transactions be treated as loans, with interest due at prevailing rates. This has the effect of reducing the value of the receivables involved. To arrive at equitable principal values for the affected receivables, imputation-of-interest calculations must be performed.

With a timesharing system it is relatively easy to develop a small program to produce figures for the imputed value of notes outstanding. With such a program, the input data will include the value of outstanding accounts receivable, which are treated as notes receivable, the interest rate appropriate for loans on this type of merchandise, and the period in which payments will be realized. The unknown is the principal value of the accounts receivable. This amount is computed and reported by the timesharing system.

As indicated earlier, potential applications of timesharing in the area of financial reporting are almost without limit. The extent to which it is used for such purposes in a particular company depends largely on the attitudes and preferences of the company's financial personnel—and, of course, on the availability of reasonably priced timesharing services.

TAX COMPUTATIONS

Tax computations can be relatively complex and error-prone. To increase the reliability of such computations, and also to relieve work pressures during busy seasons, a number of organizations have developed timesharing programs to produce Form 1040 income tax returns for individuals.

For business managers and/or public accountants, there is also considerable potential for using timesharing services in the preparation of various parts or schedules of the Form 1120 cor-

```
SCHEDULE G
(FORM 1040)          ----INCOME AVERAGING----                    1970


JOHN Q. TAXPAYER                                  123-45-6789


--------------------TAXABLE INCOME AND ADJUSTMENTS--------------------

                         (A)     (B)     (C)     (D)     (E)
                         1970    1969    1968    1967    1966
1 TAXABLE INCOME         60000   25000   20000   5000    3000
2 INCOME EARNED OUTSIDE US
  AND EXCLUDED UNDER
  SECTIONS 911 & 931     XXXXXXX  0       0       0       0
3 EXCESS COMMUNITY INCOME
  AND INCOME SUBJECT TO
  PENALTY-SEC. 72(M)(5)   0     XXXXXXX XXXXXXX XXXXXXX XXXXXXX
4 ACCUMULATION DISTRIBU-
  TIONS SUBJ TO SEC 668(A)  0     0       0       0       0
5 ADJUSTED TAXABLE INCOME
  LINE 1+LINE 2-LINES 3 & 4  60000 25000 20000   5000    3000


--------------------COMPUTATION OF AVERAGEABLE INCOME--------------------


6 ADJUSTED TAXABLE INCOME FROM LINE 5,COL(A)               60,000
7 30% OF THE SUM OF LINE 5, COLS. B,C,D,E                  15,900
8 AVERAGEABLE INCOME (LINE 6 LESS LINE 7)                  44,100


-------------------SEGMENTS OF INCOME UNDER AVERAGING-------------------


9  AMOUNT FROM LINE 7                                      15,900
10 20 PERCENT OF LINE 8                                     8,820
11 TOTAL (ADD LINES 9 & 10)                                24,720
12 AMOUNT FROM LINE 3, COL.(A), LESS ANY
   INCOME SUBJ TO PENALTY UNDER SEC. 72(M)(5)
13 TOTAL (ADD LINES 11 & 12)                               24,720


-------------------------COMPUTATION OF TAX-------------------------

14 TAX ON AMOUNT ON LINE 13                                5,919
15 TAX ON AMOUNT ON LINE 11              5,919
16 TAX ON AMOUNT ON LINE 9               3,235
17 DIFFERENCE (LINE 15 LESS LINE 16)     2,684
18 MULTIPLY THE AMOUNT ON LINE 17 BY 4                     10,736
19 TOTAL (ADD LINES 14 & 18)                               16,655
20 TAX ON INCOME SUBJ TO PENALTY-SEC 72(M)(5)
21 TAX ON ACCUM DISTRIB SUBJ TO SEC. 668(A)
22 TAX (ADD LINES 19,20 & 21)                              16,655
```

Figure 9.4 Income averaging computation.

```
          *****TAX CALCULATIONS UNDER THE TAX REFORM ACT OF 1969*****


CALCULATIONS TO BE PERFORMED:
    [NOTE: ONLY INCOME AVERAGING IS PRESENTLY AVAILABLE. OTHER CALCULATIONS
           WILL BE PROGRAMMED DURING THE NEXT FEW WEEKS]

    INCOME AVERAGING (Y OR N)...............? Y
    ALTERNATIVE CAPITAL GAINS TAX (Y OR N).? N
    MAXIMUM TAX ON EARNED INCOME (Y OR N)..? N
    TAX ON TAX PREFERENCES (Y OR N)........? N
    SECTION 72(N) TAX (Y OR N).............? N

NEW YORK STATE TAX:
    X = NOT DESIRED
    R = RESIDENT
    N = NONRESIDENT
....? X



               *****I N C O M E   A V E R A G I N G*****

               (AS REVISED BY TAX REFORM ACT OF 1969)

DETAILED INSTRUCTIONS (Y OR N)? Y

ENTER TAXPAYER NAME(S).....?JOHN C. TAXPAYER

ENTER SOCIAL SECURITY NUMBER(S).....?123-45-6789

ENTER YEAR OF COMPUTATION......? 1970

ENTER MARITAL STATUS:
    J = JOINT
    H = HEAD OF HOUSEHOLD
    M = SINGLE [1970 ONLY] OR MARRIED/SEPARATE
    S = SINGLE [AFTER 1970]
....? J

PRINT FACSIMILE SCHEDULE G (Y OR N).....? Y

SURCHARGE RATE (DECIMAL).....? .025

ENTER TAXABLE INCOME (PART I, LINE 1)
    COMPUTATION YEAR ........? 60000
    FIRST PRECEDING YEAR ...? 25000
    SECOND PRECEDING YEAR ..? 20000
    THIRD PRECEDING YEAR ...? 5000
    FOURTH PRECEDING YEAR ..? 3000

ANY SEC. 911 OR 931 INCOME EXCLUDED IN BASE PERIOD (Y OR N).....? N

ANY SEC. 72(M)(5) INCOME OR EXCESS COMMUNITY INCOME IN 1970 (Y OR N)..? N

ANY SEC. 668(A) INCOME (Y OR N)....? N



TAX WITHOUT AVERAGING
    (TAX ON    60,000,+ LINES 20 & 21)          22,300
SURCHARGE (.025)                                   557
TOTAL TAX WITHOUT AVERAGING                                  22,857

TAX - AVERAGING (LINE 22)                       16,655
SURCHARGE (.025)                                   416
TOTAL TAX - AVERAGING                                        17,071

AVERAGING SAVES                                              5,786



    ADJUSTED TAXABLE INCOME NEEDED TO BE
       ELIGIBLE FOR INCOME AVERAGNG IN 1971 IS   $   36,001
```

Figure 9.4   *(Continued)*

111

porate income tax return. Tax computations that lend themselves well to the use of timesharing programs include:

- Development of amounts of gain or loss on capital assets.
- Realization of proceeds from the sale of real property.
- Calculation of exemptions and income determination for Domestic International Sales Corporation (DISC) operations.
- Schedule G calculations of income averaging for extraordinary gains.

The calculations involved in the averaging of income will be used to illustrate opportunities for timesharing applications in the tax computation area. The program used in this illustrative example was written especially for this application, but it is general-purpose in nature—that is, it can be used for any individual taxpayer with an extraordinary-income item. The timesharing terminal transactions associated with this computation are illustrated in Figure 9.4.

Before considering how the income averaging program works, it should be recognized that its purpose is to help determine whether application of the income averaging provisions of the tax law is profitable for the individual taxpayer in the situation under consideration. Simply stated, the objective is to determine whether the taxpayer with an extraordinary-income item will reduce his tax expenses by income averaging, as compared with alternative treatments.

The timesharing program developed for this application can calculate results under income averaging, alternative capital-gains taxes, the maximum tax on earned income for the amount, and/or the taxpayer's exposure under the tax preference provisions or under Section 22(n) of the Revenue Code. On an interactive basis, the computer asks the user at the timesharing terminal to indicate which of these calculations are to be performed. It then requests specific data. In the example illustrated in Figure 9.4, the timesharing computer has determined that income averaging would save the taxpayer $5786 in taxes. If there were no saving, the computer would print out a zero for this item.

If it is decided, on the basis of this information from the computer, that the taxpayer should proceed with income averaging, the computer will print out Schedule G in a format suitable for attachment to the taxpayer's Form 1040 return.

INVESTMENT ANALYSIS

Investment analysis is an application of growing importance that combines elements of all of the techniques discussed in the preceding sections of this chapter. The main difference is that the mathematical model for investment analysis is considerably more complex than the models required for the other financial analysis applications we have considered. At the time of this writing, most programs being used for investment analysis purposes have been custom-made. This seems likely to be true for some time to come, since an effective investment analysis program must be carefully designed according to the unique characteristics or patterns of the user company's business. For almost any company there will be aspects of an investment analysis program that require a relatively large volume of repetitive computer processing, but these requirements will vary from one company to another.

Investment analysis programs must also be tailored to fit the level of sophistication of the individuals who will be using the programs and of the company's management generally. In this regard, the type of analysis undertaken is far more important than the degree of complexity or refinement built into the computer programs. Thus a company going into investment analysis with the aid of computer timesharing should look forward to a continuing process—and expense—of revising and updating its programs.

For companies that produce or distribute high-cost capital equipment, an investment analysis program can be an especially valuable tool—not only for management planning but for marketing as well. Programs can be executed from a portable terminal right in the office of a prospective customer. In just a few minutes, computer printouts of sophisticated financial analyses can be generated to support the marketing presentation. Such analyses have been used, for example, to support the payback claims of manufacturers or distributors.

In implementation, investment analysis is performed in much the same way as the financial projection application described in Chapter 8. Reports delivered to users are similar in format and level of detail to those described in that chapter. Obviously, investment analysis does not require projections of full financial statements. Investment analysis reports, however, do project the financial results of an individual project or undertaking for similar —and frequently longer—periods.

Investment analysis is typically applied to new ventures or undertakings, and the use of a computer does lend reliability to the analytical processes involved. However, a word of caution is in order: there has been an unfortunate tendency to use computer printouts for the presentation of investment analyses simply because a computer-produced document lends additional credence to a sales pitch. In effect the timesharing terminal is sometimes being used more as a "sexy" printing device than as an analytical tool.

On the positive side, prospective users should be aware of the potential value of multiple-situation analyses that can be performed easily and quickly through computer timesharing. It is possible, for example, not only to analyze whether an investment is sound but to go one step further and determine the most profitable way to structure the transaction.

A good illustration of an investment analysis application is a real estate development company specializing in multi-unit residential property. The company builds apartment houses, manages the completed structures, then sells them at a time when they have achieved the company's investment objectives and are also potentially profitable for institutional investors. Inputs to this investment analysis program include:

- Cost of the property.
- Cost of improvements to the property.
- Depreciable life of the property.
- Depreciation method.
- Income tax bracket of the investor for whom the analysis is being performed.
- Projected revenues from use of the property.

- A forecasted vacancy factor.
- Operating costs.
- Percentages of ownership of partners.
- Projected year of disposal and sale price.

From these data, the computer develops reports that show the yield for each partner, on a pretax and after-tax basis. In addition, each partner receives a detailed schedule of cash flow, by year, for the full life of every product.

In establishing this program, the developers were, in effect, committing themselves to realize the projected results. In a speculative business, they were subjecting themselves to a high degree of accountability. This, in turn, helped make their projects more attractive to prospective investors.

Note the similarity between the capital budgeting application described earlier and this investment analysis program. The approach and formats are quite similar. Obviously, however, the investment analysis program includes far more parameters. The results produced by the investment analysis program are intended to be much more definitive than what is normally required for capital budgeting purposes.

With consideration of the investment analysis application, it becomes apparent that there can be strong tie-ins between the financial analysis and financial projection functions within a company. In some cases the results of financial analysis applications can contribute directly to the data base used in financial projections. And the same characteristics of relatively low volume and one-time utilization apply to both financial analysis and projecttion. Thus both types of applications lend themselves well to the use of computer timesharing. In each case risk is low, costs are known early in each project, and the consequences of discontinuance of efforts are relatively minor.

10 Operational
Applications

Historically, line operating management has been slow to accept and use the concepts and techniques of management analysis and planning. Line operations have traditionally been strongholds of "seat-of-the-pants" management. Top operational managers have tended to gain their positions on the basis of extensive experience, typically within one industry and often through extended tenure with a single company. As a result there has been much less cross-fertilization, from industry to industry and company to company, in line operating management than in financial management and other corporate staff functions, in which both management people and management concepts have been more mobile.

The past 15 or 20 years, however, have seen a gradual but accelerating change in this situation. Line operations have been subjected increasingly to the concepts and techniques of quantitative analysis and computer-assisted planning and control. As in other areas of computer application, government and big business have led the way, through the development of simplified computer languages and programs for simulation, scheduling, and statistical analysis.

Ultimately these software tools found their way into timesharing libraries. As people moved between jobs—and as more and more college graduates familiar with these new concepts and techniques moved into industry—the use of quantitative analysis by line operating management increased accordingly. Today it is safe to say that operationally oriented quantitative analysis applications represent a significant portion of overall business timesharing utilization. And this is an application area that promises to continue to grow in the foreseeable future.

AN OVERVIEW

The characteristics of operational applications of timesharing are similar to those of the other analytical applications discussed in Chapters 7 through 9. That is, the applications tend to be of a one-time nature; they tend to entail large volumes of computer processing but relatively small volumes of printed output; and users tend to be relatively sophisticated. Again, the nature of these applications is such that management knows, very early in the process of preparing for an application, what its commitments and costs will be. And programs can be discontinued or scrapped with relatively little impact on the company's business. As is also true of most of the management analysis applications described in the preceding chapters, standard programming languages and packages for operational applications have become widely available in timesharing utilities' libraries.

Thus the major distinguishing characteristic of operational applications is the fact that they impact the operational—as distinct from the purely financial—areas of a company's business.

To provide a general understanding of how timesharing is used in operational applications, three common types of applications are described briefly here:

- Project scheduling and control.
- Simulation modeling.
- Statistical analysis and forecasting.

PROJECT SCHEDULING AND CONTROL

Simply defined, project scheduling and control is a technique for managing developmental efforts—for forecasting and staying on top of the untried or the unknown. By its nature, a "project" represents a new undertaking for the particular organizations involved. Computerized project scheduling and control techniques were first used, for example, in the development of weapons systems for the U.S. Navy. In many ways, the development of a weapons system epitomizes the characteristics of a project: the end result desired by management is known; the general steps to be taken can be delineated; but there are so many events between the start and completion of the project that it is impossible, without some special assistance, to predict bottlenecks or problems on an intuitive basis. The most popular computer-assisted technique for identifying and controlling project activities—and the relationships between such activities—is the critical-path method (CPM).

The critical-path method is a structured, often-computerized technique that is designed to define and analyze data provided by project managers on the activities and events leading to completion of the project. Computer outputs become a tool for identifying and analyzing conflicts in schedules, availability of resources, constraints associated with the project, and other key project management considerations.

As critical-path programs have become available through time-sharing services, they have been adopted by many companies with project-type organizations or activities. One good example is a building contractor. If such a company has a contract to build a major new factory, for example, management can identify a series of events or activities necessary to the completion of the project, beginning with the acquisition and clearing of the land and ending with the actual occupancy of the completed factory. Between these two points, the necessary activities or events will fall logically into a series of parallel paths or sequences. Grading, for example, must be completed before cement can be poured; cement must be poured before framing can take place; framing must be completed before wiring can begin. For each such activity, projections can be made of the length of time it will take and its sequence in the project—that is, what other activities must be completed before it can be initiated.

Timesharing programs for critical-path planning are designed to identify that continuous sequence of events that will take the longest time to complete. This, then, becomes the "critical path." A computer is valuable in this process because it is able to test all of the alternatives or combinations of activities associated with a project to identify the critical path. This can easily require tens of thousands—even hundreds of thousands—of specific tests and comparisons to identify the set of events critical to project completion. Even on relatively small projects, performance of all these tests and comparisons quickly exceeds the limits of manual processing capabilities. The use of computer timesharing services is especially convenient, since standardized programs to perform all of these tests and comparisons are readily available at the other end of a telephone dial.

A critical-path network is shown in Figure 10.1. This type of network is a graphic representation of data derived from a computer printout. A typical printout used to develop—and periodically modify or update—charts like the one in Figure 10.1 is shown in Figure 10.2.

The utilization of critical-path techniques is usually determined by and under the control of the manager of the particular project concerned. The methodology is similar for a wide range of project areas—construction, research, product development, system development, and so on. By their nature, projects of this type will involve varying numbers of people and other resources at different stages. Administratively, one person is frequently given responsibility for scheduling and feedback reporting of progress. This individual, even if he has no data-processing background, is usually quantitativiely oriented. Typically, he can learn enough about timesharing to implement computerized critical-path scheduling and control with a small amount of training.

Functionally, the major task involved in the use of timesharing for computer-assisted critical-path analysis and planning is to format the input data from the supervisors or managers of the various activities so that it is compatible with the requirements of the program to be used. Once this input has been properly formatted, it is relatively simple to derive the reports that serve as a basis for the development of critical-path networks. The major challenge, however, lies in applying critical-path techniques consistently. Unless critical-path networks and reports are maintained on a current basis, they quickly lose value—and may become dangerously misleading. One of the major problems encountered in the use of critical-path techniques is the tendency to create a carefully developed network at the outset of a project but then fail to maintain it on a current basis. Too often, reports are not collected regularly, the network is not updated, and the

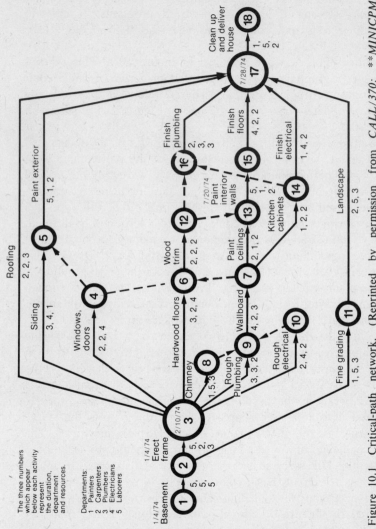

Figure 10.1 Critical-path network. (Reprinted by permission from *CALL/370:* **MINICPM,** **MAXICPM** *Critical Path Scheduling,* copyright © 1973 by The Service Bureau Company, a division of Control Data Corporation.)

120

AUTOMATIC UPDATE SUMMARY

EARLY START DATES

WORK TO BE COMPLETED BETWEEN 1/ 4/74 AND 2/16/74

PRED EVENT	SUCC EVENT	DEPT	DESCRIPTION	TIME REMAINING AS OF 1/ 4/74	AS OF 2/16/74	STATUS
1	2	5	POUR BASEMENT	5.0	0.0	
2	3	2	ERECT FRAME	5.0	0.0	
2	11	5	FINE GRADING	1.0	0.0	
3	4	2	WINDOWS DOORS	2.0	0.0	
3	5	4	SIDING	3.0	0.0	
3	6	2	HARDWOOD FLOORS	3.0	0.0	
3	8	5	CHIMNEY	1.0	0.0	
3	9	3	ROUGH PLUMBING	3.0	0.0	CRITICAL
3	10	4	ROUGH ELECTRICAL	2.0	0.0	
3	17	2	ROOFING	2.0	0.0	
5	17	1	PAINT EXTERIOR	5.0	4.0	
9	7	2	WALLBOARD	4.0	3.0	CRITICAL
11	17	5	LANDSCAPE	2.0	0.0	

TOTAL NUMBER OF IN-PROCESS ACTIVITIES EQUALS 13
2   OF THESE ARE CRITICAL

CURRENT START DATE: 1/ 4/74

COMPLETION DATE: 3/ 9/74

REMAINING WORK DAYS TO COMPLETE PROJECT: 46

Figure 10.2 Timesharing printout used to develop, modify, or update critical-path network. (Reprinted by permission from *CALL/370: **MINICPM, **MAXICPM Critical Path Scheduling,* copyright © 1973 by The Service Bureau Company, a division of Control Data Corporation.)

project managers assume that control exists when, in fact, it may have been lost during the first month, when the system was not kept up to date.

Managers considering the use of critical-path techniques with the assistance of timesharing systems should be aware that the value of such applications depends heavily upon continuity and follow-through.

SIMULATION MODELING

Simulation modeling is a technique for examining the effects and results of projected or hypothetical operations as a basis for management decisions on how things are to be done. It is used, in general, either to test new ways of performing established functions or to test alternative ways of performing an operation that is under consideration or in development.

Simulation modeling is now supported routinely by appropriate programming languages available through timesharing utilities. In each case, however, the specific program or model of the function to be simulated must be developed individually. Thus some mathematical and data-processing expertise is necessary for the development of simulation modeling applications. This is, in fact, perhaps the most sophisticated application of timesharing discussed in this book. In short, simulation modeling is no place for the novice to plunge in without qualified technical assistance or staff expertise.

The models used in this type of application are referred to as "probabilistic." The approach is also known as "Monte Carlo analysis" because of the obvious parallel to gambling situations in attempting to determine the probability of occurrence of simulated events. In applying simulation modeling programs, users enter probability data, expressed as ranges of possible occurrence, as inputs.

One classic, and very simple, illustration of simulation modeling is planning for checkout services in a supermarket. Assumptions are made about the frequency of arrival of customers and the length of time needed for customers to process their purchases through a checkout counter. Assumptions are also made about the number of checkout lanes that will be open.

Processing of the simulation problem produces results on the average wait-in-line per customer at different times of day and/or different days of the week. Management can then compare these results with figures representing the level of service it wishes to provide to customers. The basic premise is that there are reasonable limits to the amount of time customers will wait in line at checkstands before they begin to try another supermarket. If a simulation run on a timesharing computer shows that checkstand waiting lines are longer than these standards, management can then analyze—and place a value on—the amount of business likely to be lost. This value can then be compared with the cost of adding additional checkstands and/or additional personnel to process customer purchases faster. The results attainable by adding more checkstands and/or personnel can then be tested through further simulation on the timesharing computer.

As this example suggests, simulation modeling is generally used to gain a better understanding of real-world situations. Typically, a manager is confronted with a specific operating problem and wants to explore several alternative approaches for resolving the problem. Simulation modeling gives him an opportunity to identify and compare the results that can reasonably be expected from each of the alternatives under consideration.

Other frequently cited examples of simulation modeling are applications in the area of transportation planning—scheduling passenger or cargo operations for railroads, trucking companies, airlines, and the like; designing materials-handling systems and shipping and receiving facilities for a new plant; or determining the number of automatic elevators required in a high-rise office building: how many elevators should service each "bank" of floors, what the optimal combinations of floor banks are, and so on.

Managers considering the use of simulation modeling should keep in mind that the value of such techniques is limited by their (i.e., the managers') own ability to predict, with some degree of confidence, the probable impact on their operations of various kinds of change. If a manager does not really know or understand the factors that determine the volume, capacity, and other characteristics of his operations, it is unlikely that he will be able to input sufficiently reliable probability estimates to develop realistic projections from a simulation modeling program.

In general, simulation modeling is most useful in situations where management can determine or predict, within realistic ranges, the volume or frequency of key variables affecting the operation in question under various assumed conditions. In other words, the better that management itself can predict the results of a particular change in operations, the more valuable simulation modeling can be as a tool to refine, test, and extend such predictions.

STATISTICAL ANALYSIS AND FORECASTING

Statistical analysis and forecasting includes a number of techniques that operating management can and does use as decision-making aids in a variety of applications. In this brief review, we limit our consideration to two of the most widely publicized (and perhaps least widely understood) applications of statistical analysis and forecasting:

1. Predicting future results or trends on the basis of past history ("regression analysis").
2. Determining the characteristics or composition of a large group of things or people—a "universe," as the statisticians call it—on the basis of information about only a small fraction of the total group ("statistical sampling").

Although many operating managers profess to be bewildered by "sophisticated" mathematical techniques, neither of these two applications is so complex or difficult as its name may suggest. Sandardized programs capable of performing complete regression analyses are available from many timesharing utilities, and a number of statistical sampling functions can be performed with programs available in timesharing libraries.

The practicality of these applications can be illustrated by a familiar example. Wide publicity has been given to the prediction of election returns on the basis of patterns of past results from selected, representative districts. The computer programs that generate these predictions use a combination of regression analysis and statistical sampling techniques: regression analysis to predict future outcomes from past results; statistical sampling to select those districts that are representative of the whole universe of voters.

Election forecasting was initiated in 1952, by the computer industry itself, using large-scale, dedicated computer systems. Gradually, as the methodology proved appropriate elsewhere, individual companies applied similar methods, using their own computers, to forecasting problems associated with their own business problems and objectives. Ultimately, timesharing utilities began to offer the same basic capabilities to many users on a standardized basis.

Regression Analysis Applications

Timesharing users can, for example, apply regression analysis techniques in developing sales forecasts for future periods. Purchasing histories—and trends—for each of the company's products, by type of customer, can be used to develop reliable predictions of sales by product, territory, and the like. This process can be refined—and, in many cases, made more reliable—by considering various characteristics of the company's customer population. For example, analyses can be made that consider such characteristics as age, economic status, and geographic shifts in population. When regression analysis is performed on the basis of a series of factors or characteristics, the process is known as "multiple-regression analysis."

To illustrate the process of multiple-regression analysis, consider the situation of an oil company choosing locations for service stations. Existing locations would be analyzed and classified according to degree of success. The locations themselves would then be analyzed according to traffic, accessibility, competition in the immediate area, population density, general economic level of the neighborhood, mix of residential and business sites, and many other factors. It is possible to identify literally dozens of characteristics that correlate to a profile of success in the selection of future service station locations and their design.

In processing such an analysis on a timesharing computer, the user would begin by entering sales statistics for all of the existing locations to be analyzed. (For a large company, this input might represent a sampling of the total number of locations.) As a next step, values would be entered for each of the characteristics to be used in the analysis, for every station. Under the control of a standardized timesharing program, the computer would deliver reports indicating for each of the characteristics a "coefficient of correlation" reflecting its contribution to the success of a service station location. These coefficients of correlation would be evaluated according to their degree of importance in achieving business success at individual locations.

Caution: Problems can arise from attempts to use regression analysis techniques with insufficient data. If, for example, a company operated 100 service stations in a given market area, the coefficient-of-correlation figures developed on the basis of data from three or four locations in this area would not be sufficiently reliable to serve as the basis for decisions. In such a case, reliable figures would require data covering perhaps 30 or more locations.

Statistical Sampling Applications

A familiar example of the use of statistical sampling techniques in business is the test-marketing of new products. It has become common practice to introduce new products on a limited basis in markets with well-known characteristics—characteristics that also apply to broader geographic areas or population segments. Given information on the population and other factors associated with the test market—and given the results of the test-marketing efforts—projections can be made, by statistical sampling, of the probable total market for the new product.

The development of test-marketing samples through the use of timesharing is both practical and profitable. Packaged programs for the development of samples are among the most popular services offered by timesharing utilities.

Another business area in which statistical sampling is widely applied is inventory valuation and management. Consider, for example, a company that has between 30,000 and 40,000 items of inventory in stock. Management wants to know whether the return on its investment in inventories can be improved. Under one inventory analysis program developed by the authors' firm, Arthur Young & Company, and known as "TRIM" (Technique for Review of Inventory Management), the user starts simply by entering the number of items in stock and the level of confidence desired in the projection based on the sample. The program assumes a sequential numbering of inventory items in line with the company's stock numbering system. From just these two items of input, the program generates both the size of the sample and a list of items to be included in the sample.

For each item in the sample, the user then gathers and enters a number of parameters, including the following:

- Cumulative usage.
- Time period for the usage.
- Number of orders placed.
- Unit cost.
- Number of withdrawals from inventory.
- Number of times the item has been out of stock when ordered.
- Balance on hand.
- Balance on hand at date of last reorder.
- Lead time for replenishment (in working days).
- Order cost or setup cost.
- Carrying charge for keeping the item in stock.

From this information, the computer generates a detailed report analyzing the total inventory. A typical report is shown in Figure 10.3. In the example illustrated, analysis has shown that the company could reduce its inventory by 31.6 percent without compromising the levels of service established by management. The potential reduction in inventory investment is $72,882.

BEYOND SCIENTIFIC MANAGEMENT

The applications and techniques described in this chapter are frequently referred to, collectively, by such catchall terms as "operations research," "management sciences," or "scientific management." The use of such vague and general labels in itself says something about the way that management has traditionally

PART NUMBER	ANNUAL DOLLAR USAGE IN DESCENDING ORDER	DOLLAR VALUE OF ACTUAL INVENTORY	DOLLAR VALUE OF SUGGESTED AVERAGE INVENTORY	INVENTORY EXCEEDING SUGGESTED AVERAGE LEVEL	EXCESS INVENTORY
46	1660.80	332	923	-591	
20	1102.20	33	377	-344	
11	599.20	0	186	-186	
25	560.00	345	313	32	
50	497.70	59	681	-622	
42	408.80	285	240	45	
31	365.60	320	196	124	38
23	292.60	355	168	187	111
30	282.15	219	190	29	
43	244.08	705	115	590	520
8	237.60	79	192	-113	
5	187.00	37	125	-88	
15	174.18	29	130	-101	
52	166.65	182	120	62	4
24	124.15	25	117	-92	
48	120.54	214	69	145	96
55	114.25	183	109	74	26
26	114.19	30	180	-150	
3	111.50	22	107	-85	
39	104.50	31	165	-134	
32	93.73	428	86	342	299
7	91.97	32	68	-36	
9	73.77	639	93	546	508
19	66.00	33	112	-79	
33	65.11	11	111	-100	
49	43.71	148	48	100	70
44	41.30	1012	59	953	924
35	40.44	404	58	346	318
13	40.17	228	58	170	141
2	39.00	16	37	-21	
27	38.50	6	73	-67	
36	34.30	15	42	-27	
4	32.24	16	41	-25	
53	30.00	62	50	12	
22	24.36	171	34	137	114
40	19.80	42	24	18	
54	10.00	130	22	108	94
41	7.00	23	15	8	
34	5.92	18	14	4	
10	4.55	0	13	-13	
28	1.09	69	5	64	59
6	1.07	15	5	10	5
18	0.	10	0	10	10
38	0.	58	0	58	58
45	0.	22	0	22	22
1	0.	5	0	5	5
47	0.	7	0	7	7
16	0.	866	0	866	866
21	0.	53	0	53	53
12	0.	13	0	13	13
51	0.	48	0	48	48
14	0.	22	0	22	22
29	0.	47	0	47	47
37	0.	67	0	67	67
17	0.	221	0	221	221
SAMPLE TOTALS	8271.72	8444	5772	2672	4767

Figure 10.3 "TRIM" inventory analysis report (Arthur Young & Company).

128

TOTAL INVENTORY VALUES	DOLLAR VALUE OF ACTUAL INVENTORY	DOLLAR VALUE OF SUGGESTED AVERAGE INVENTORY	INVENTORY EXCEEDING SUGGESTED AVERAGE LEVEL	EXCESS INVENTORY
HIGH	287270	199126	139672	180160
ESTIMATED	230294	157412	72882	130022
LOW	173318	115698	6092	79883

TOTAL INVENTORY VALUES ARE BASED ON A 80.0 % CONFIDENCE LEVEL

CONCLUSIONS:
    BASED ON USING EOQ RULES THE POTENTIAL REDUCTION OF
    INVENTORY WOULD BE AN EXPECTED VALUE OF   72882.
    THIS IS A REDUCTION OF   31.6 PERCENT.

Figure 10.3 (*Continued*)

regarded the use of computers in general, and timesharing techniques specifically, for operational applications. The fact that the
names are becoming more specific and the applications better
delineated indicates that both use of and knowledge about these
methods are increasing rapidly. Collectively or individually, these
operational applications of timesharing offer high potential returns
on limited investments to companies that use them judiciously.

11 Getting Started
in Timesharing

For experienced managers, the decision process associated with the introduction of timesharing services within a company should be both familiar and easy to follow. In essence, the decision to use timesharing, whether for record-keeping or problem-solving applications, involves a commitment of company resources.

A proven pattern for managing such a commitment might run along these lines:

1. Assign responsibility for managing the initiation of a time-sharing system, including responsibility for all of the following steps.
2. Define the project objectives clearly and develop benchmarks for testing out project costs.
3. Evaluate and compare the facilities and capabilities of qualified suppliers.
4. Evaluate supplier services, including customer support, training and guidance of user personnel, and reliability of the time-sharing utility itself.
5. Estimate, as closely as possible, the total expense involved in initiating and carrying on the timesharing activity, including consideration of such matters as whether to rent or buy terminal equipment; such frequently overlooked costs as system design and programming; and the cost impact of the processing approach (i.e., interactive vs. remote batch).
6. Consider alternative techniques, and their associated costs, for handling the same job or equipment other than timesharing computers—that is, electronic bookkeeping machines, mini-computers, programmable electronic calculators, and so on.
7. If, after the initial feasibility evaluations of timesharing utility capabilities and costs, it is decided to go ahead and one or

more timesharing vendors are chosen, proceed with system design and development activities no less thorough and professional than you would require for an in-house computer installation.

In the pages that follow we consider each of these steps at greater length.

ASSIGNING RESPONSIBILITY

Whatever the scope or magnitude of the timesharing activity that a company may be contemplating, responsibility for managing that activity should be clearly defined. Where such responsibility is assigned and how it is exercised will, of course, vary according to the size of the company, the nature of its operations, and its existing commitment to, and organization for, data processing.

If, for example, the company already has a systems and procedures group within its data-processing department, this would, in most cases, be a logical place to assign responsibility for the initiation of a timesharing program. In other cases, the company's management style may call for a sharing of responsibilities between a systems analyst and a manager from the using department (or, if there is to be more than one using department, from each of the departments involved). In still other cases, responsibility may reside entirely with an operating-level manager in the using department. In any case, the manager assigned responsibility for the timesharing effort should have a clear understanding of what results he is expected to deliver, what resources will be available, and the time frame involved.

An important consideration associated with the establishment of project responsibility is the availability of qualified technical support within the company. If responsibility is assigned to an experienced systems analyst, there should be no problem in this regard. If responsibility is assigned to or assumed by a manager with little previous data-processing experience, however, it will be necessary to make some provision for technical support. If possible, someone with appropriate data-processing or timesharing experience—perhaps someone who used timesharing systems at college—should be assigned to assist the responsible manager. If such a person is not available, the manager may require enough lead time to educate himself to a level necessary to evaluate alternatives and arrive at an intelligent decision. (One of the authors' main purposes in writing this book was to provide a brief but comprehensive "primer" for managers who find themselves in this position.)

Another alternative, which has been followed by many companies preparing to use timesharing for the first time, is to engage a consultant to establish criteria, select the vendors, and launch the program. Even the best consulting services are not a panacea, however. If a consultant is engaged, the company should be prepared ultimately to develop its own capability for managing and operating its timesharing program.

DEFINING OBJECTIVES
AND DEVELOPING BENCHMARKS

Once responsibility for managing the timesharing program has been assigned, the first requirement is that project objectives be defined clearly for the benefit of both the company's management and prospective vendors.

The responsible manager should begin by defining all end-product reports and/or documents to be generated by the timesharing system. He should then define the inputs that will be made available to achieve those results and, in general terms, the processing that is to take place. These specifications should be clear enough and detailed enough that they can be used as the basis for proposals by timesharing utilities and for value-based decisions by managers within the user company.

At this early stage it is not necessary that the responsible manager undertake a complete system design effort. Rather, he should outline the project as a whole, in general terms. He should also take one small but representative segment of the project and outline it in enough specific detail that it can serve as an actual test of performance. In data-processing circles, this type of limited test problem is known as a "benchmark" problem. Typically, benchmark problems are given to several prospective vendors, who then base their proposals and cost projections on their experience in processing the benchmark problems.

Thus, as his first actions, the responsible manager should outline the system to be developed and prepare a benchmark performance test covering one representative segment of the work to be done.

EVALUATING SUPPLIERS' FACILITIES AND CAPABILITIES

Evaluation of the qualifications of potential sources of the required timesharing services should begin as soon as possible after responsibility for the timesharing activity has been assigned. Basically this procedure consists of (1) identifying the timesharing utilities that may be able to provide the required services and (2) evaluating and comparing their facilities and capabilities. Obviously this effort will be largely technical in nature.

Sources of information about timesharing suppliers abound— from the Yellow Pages to your accountants, your bankers, or your friend Joe Whatzisname at Company Z, down the turnpike. One useful reference is the survey report, *All About Remote Computing Services,* prepared each year by Datapro Research Corporation.* Through the kind permission of Datapro Research, we have included the most recent address listing of 97 leading timesharing suppliers, and a table indicating the types of application programs available from them, as Appendix A of this book. The complete annual survey report contains a great deal more detailed information about each of the suppliers. An example of the kind of information included in this report is shown in Figure 11.1.

Facilities

The most important considerations in evaluating the facilities of a timesharing utility are the size and configuration of the com-

---

* This annual survey report was formerly called *All About Computer Timesharing Services.* The name was changed in the most recent edition, published in December 1973, to reflect the fact that the report now covers the full spectrum of computer services available to users at remote terminals— including both interactive timesharing services and remote batch-processing services.

COMPANY	Tymshare, Inc.	Uni-Coll	United Computing Systems, Inc.	University Computing Company
GENERAL				
Name of service	TYMCOM IX, X, & 370	TSO and APL at Uni-Coll	UCS	1108/FASBAC services
Date operational	1966	July 1970	Jan. 1968	May 1969
Areas currently served	Local access in all major U.S. metropolitan areas, plus INWATS; local access in London, Paris, & Brussels	Delaware Valley	Major metropolitan areas nationwide thru network of multiplexers; national INWATS for remote batch; expanding to major Canadian cities	Entire U.S. (thru WATS and multiplexers), plus England, Western Europe and Australia
EQUIPMENT				
Computers	Xerox 940 (26), DEC PDP-10 (6), & IBM 370/158 (1); in Cupertino, CA & other locations	IBM 370/168 & DECsystem-10 (KI) in Philadelphia	CDC Cyber 70 (3), CDC 6600, & CDC 6500 in Kansas City, Mo.	UNIVAC 1108's in Dallas (4), East Brunswick, N.J. (2), London (2), and Sydney
No. of simultaneous users	1500 total	110 total	Proprietary	FASBAC: 25 per system
Conversational terminals supported	Any ASCII, EBCDIC, or Correspondence unit at 10, 15, or 30 cps, in full or half duplex mode	Any ASCII unit at 10, 30, or 120 cps; IBM 2741 & compatible units at 14.8 cps	Virtually all 10 to 30 cps terminals (120 cps in 1975)	ASCII, EBCDIC, & Correspondence units at 10, 15, or 30 cps
Batch terminals supported	IBM 2780 and compatible units	Any HASP-compatible RJE terminal	Data 100, DEC PDP-11, Mohawk 2400, Remcom, UNIVAC 1004, etc.	Any unit capable of operating in UNIVAC 1004 or COPE mode
SOFTWARE				
Conversational programming language	FORTRAN, BASIC, COBOL, PL/1, Assembler, Editor	APL & TSO on IBM 370/168; FORTRAN, BASIC, COBOL, ALGOL, APL on DECsystem-10	FORTRAN, BASIC, Editor	CASH, CALC, SHOBOL, Fastext
Batch-mode programming languages	–	FORTRAN, COBOL, PL/1, RPG, Assembler on IBM 370/168	FORTRAN, BASIC, COBOL, ALGOL, Compass, Simscript	FORTRAN, COBOL, ALGOL, Assembly
Principal applications	Business & scientific	Academic, scientific, administrative	Business & scientific	Business & scientific
CHARGES				
Min. monthly charge:				
Interactive	$80	None	$100	None
Remote batch	None	None	$100	None
Terminal connect time:				
Interactive	$16/hr.	$3.60/hr. (168)	$10.50-37.50/hr.	$8.50-11.00/hr.
Remote batch	–	None	$10.00-30.00/hr.	$3.00/hr.
Central processor time:				
Interactive	$0.05/sec.	$45.00/min. (168)	$1.50-36.00/min.	$1.10/1000 CRU's
Remote batch	–	$27.00-58.50/min.	$9.60-33.60/min.	Not specified
Mass storage:				
Interactive	$0.50-1.00/1000 chars./month	$0.02/13,000 chars./day	$0.50/1280 chars./month	$1.00/2048 chars./month
Remote batch	–	$0.02/13,000 chars./day	$50.00/204,800 chars./month	$0.14/7K 36-bit words/day
COMMENTS	Charges shown are for Type A service on Xerox 940; other service plans are available; operates an extensive international network called TYMNET; over 600 employees	Offers System/370 RJE, TSO, & APL services and DECsystem-10 time-sharing services to educational and commercial customers	Offers variety of pricing options and 4 levels of service: time-sharing, remote batch, RJE (batch job entry from TS environment), and local batch	Principal emphasis is on remote batch processing; FASBAC is an interactive batch system, offered at a maximum hourly rate of $17/hr.

Figure 11.1 Example of detailed information about timesharing suppliers available from the annual survey report, *All About Remote Computing Services.* (Reprinted by permission. Copyright © 1975 by Datapro Research Corporation.)

puter itself. Not to be overlooked, however, are such other considerations as the performance record of the utility, the communication systems and equipment used, and the peripheral devices available.

The prime objective is to evaluate the efficiency with which the user's specific job will be processed on the computer systems and through the communication lines, terminals, and peripheral devices used by the utility in question. Interruptions or malfunctions of communication links are an especially common cause of failure in timesharing systems. The manager evaluating a particular timesharing service should talk to people in other companies who are using the same terminal and communications equipment. He should ask for information about the kinds of interruptions or failures they have experienced, their consequences, and recovery alternatives available through the timesharing service.

The next, and perhaps the most important, factor to be considered is the response time or turnaround capability of the processing equipment used by the utility. An effective way to test the turnaround capability of the timesharing utility is to run the benchmark problem developed at the outset of the timesharing project. To the extent possible, this benchmark problem should be run under the same circumstances and conditions that would characterize the rest of the timesharing work to be done. These conditions include, for example, the time of day, the number of transactions entered in a typical time period, and the amount and complexity of the processing required.

In making this evaluation, the prospective user should expect to encounter wide variations among the makes and models of computers used by timesharing services. Of more importance than make and model to the user, however, is *how his job will be performed within his specific time and cost constraints*. In most cases, timesharing decisions are made on the basis of tradeoffs between performance (including turnaround time) and cost. Thus, while the performance available from a given supplier should be evaluated carefully, it must be weighed against the related cost of service.

The facilities of a timesharing utility should also be evaluated in terms of file capacities and file-handling capabilities. The prospective user should estimate the size of the files that will be generated to support his own application. If, for example, the company is performing financial projections for 50 accounts, covering 16 quarters, with each projection figure carried to seven digits, the file requirement for this application will be 50 times 16 times 7, or 5600 character positions. Similar computations should be performed for the more extensive file requirements that would be entailed in a large record-keeping application. Functionally, the objective is to evaluate the physical capabilities or limitations of the utility's files that could affect the usability of the system. File size will also have a significant impact on the cost of timesharing services.

Capabilities

The capabilities of a timesharing utility have to do with such things as the quality of the software used, the types of programming languages available, and the file access techniques employed. These considerations will be more important to the company contemplating problem-solving applications than to the company contemplating record-keeping applications.

The software employed in a timesharing system is particularly important where the system will be used on an interactive basis. The system software identifies users and provides most of the security and privacy controls associated with system utilization. Accordingly, the prospective user should examine the system software to the degree necessary to satisfy himself as to the degreee of protection that will be afforded to his programs and information files.

The programming languages available from a particular timesharing utility can be critically important to a problem-solving user, and the programming capabilities of individual systems should be examined in some depth. For example, BASIC is the most commonly used language for the processing of problem-solving applications on timesharing systems. However, there are many different versions of BASIC, depending on both the manufacturer and the size of the computer involved. An unsuspecting user might, for example, find that a timesharing utility offers only a limited number of program commands in its (i.e., the user company's) own version of BASIC. Such a limitation could significantly reduce the value of a timesharing service—for example, by making it impossible for the company to use programs that may have been developed for use on a computer with a larger BASIC command vocabulary.

Conversely, the user should be aware that if he initiates timesharing service with a sophisticated programming language offering a wide variety of commands, it may be difficult to change at a later date and run existing programs on other systems. Thus the consequences of programming-language selection should be considered from a number of vantage points, with the decision based on the realities of the user's situation and the capabilities and reliability of the timesharing service.

Any user whose potential applications may require the writing of special programs should investigate the various utilities' capabilities for incremental compiling of programs. Such capabilities are particularly valuable to those who are novices at programming or who program only occasionally. Under this approach, each line of coding entered by a terminal user is compiled into machine language as soon as the instruction has been typed into the terminal. If the line of program coding contains an error, the compilation will detect this error and produce a diagnostic message indicating the nature of the problem. Incremental compiling makes program writing easier and, in most cases, faster. Therefore, a prospective timesharing user who will be doing his own programming should determine whether incremental compiling capabilities are available.

A user considering record-keeping applications should carefully evaluate the standardized programs offered. The considerations involved in such an evaluation were discussed in Chapter 4. Basically, the user's concern should be with the degree of compromise or modification required in his company's normal procedures to accommodate to the constraints or limitations of a standardized timesharing program.

Also important to the user evaluating the capabilities of a timesharing utility is the range of file access techniques which can be implemented. As discussed in Chapter 3, the two basic methods for accessing data files stored in computers are (1) direct access and (2) sequential reference. With direct access, the computer is able to seek and use exactly the record it needs, referring to massive files on a random-order basis. Sequential processing requires that records within a file be read in order, starting with the beginning and searching in sequence to find the desired data.

For many record-keeping applications, particularly order-entry or inventory accounting jobs, direct-access capabilities are virtually essential. In addition, a problem-solving user will want direct-access capabilities if he plans to change individual parameters or data elements within the various models to be run on the computer. Obviously, a direct-access capability in such a situation eliminates the need to review or reenter complete files of data to change just one element.

In considering the file management capabilities of one or more timesharing utilities, the user may come across the term "virtual memory." The user's interest in virtual memory will center chiefly on the potential contribution that this capability can make in reducing response time. With the virtual memory, a computer treats a portion of its peripheral files, usually drums or disks, as though they were part of the main memory of the processor. User programs in particular are "swapped" between virtual- and main-memory locations at high speeds. This can have the effect of minimizing response time delays as a timesharing computer shifts back and forth between segments of user jobs. The average user will not have to concern himself with the details of how virtual memory is implemented. Since any prospective user of timesharing services is almost sure to hear this term referred to, however, it would seem desirable to understand the concept well enough to put the claims of prospective suppliers in proper perspective.

EVALUATING SUPPLIER SERVICES

Evaluating the services offered by a timesharing utility can be just as important to the user as evaluating its physical facilities and capabilities. Such an evaluation should include:

- Application and customer support services for users of standardized programs.
- Training and guidance for user personnel doing their own programming.
- Reliability of the timesharing utility itself—particularly as it affects prospective continuity of operation.
- Suppliers' commitments and interests, as they may affect the operating continuity of the user's timesharing applications.

Application and Customer Support

Application support services can be a make-or-break factor for a company considering the installation of a packaged record-keeping system offered by a timesharing utility. Typically, time-sharing utilities in this field provide systems support, including the development of procedures and the design of forms necessary to create input for their systems. For a company making the transition from manual procedures to computerized operations for the first time with timesharing, the system development require-ments can be substantial. If the company has not previously experienced the discipline associated with mechanized bookkeep-ing, for example, the structuring of input records on transmittal forms and the setting up of procedures with accompanying manuals can range from the difficult to the traumatic. At very least, a representative of the timesharing utility should spend the necessary time with the prospective user to clarify the system requirements that must be met and advise the user on the alternatives available to him for meeting those requirements.

In addition, a timesharing service offering standardized program packages should be expected to have facilities and qualified personnel available to train members of the user company's staff. An obvious area in which training is usually necessary is instruc-tion in how to operate a terminal. In addition, some training may be necessary in the concepts and design of the manual systems that will support the timesharing application.

The manager of a company contemplating the use of a standardized program through a timesharing utility should be aware that failures in the people part of any computerized system can be both more damaging and more costly than any mechanical problems that may be encountered. The extent and the depth of the timesharing utility's commitment in these areas should be evaluated critically and carefully.

Programming Support

Programming support services are of special importance to users contemplating problem-solving applications. The timesharing utility must have adequate training courses available for user personnel who will be doing their own programming. Ideally, such courses should be available at different levels. Thus a person already experienced in programming might need just a few hours of training on the specific terminal and equipment he will be using. On the other hand, a novice will have to begin with basics and build his skill more gradually. It would obviously be wasteful if the experienced programmer had to sit through a training course designed for novices.

For all programming trainees, courses should include practice in diagnosing problems. Where incremental compiling is done, the system generates diagnostic messages in response to erroneous entries. Each trainee should gain enough practice in encountering and responding to diagnostic messages that he will not be flustered needlessly when he encounters such messages in his company's application.

Another requirement in the programming area is the availability of experienced programmers employed by the timesharing service for consultation on problems encountered by the user. After minimal initial training, user personnel may still be novices as timesharing programmers. Occasionally, any programmer is likely to encounter a problem, or a system reaction, with which his training has not prepared him to deal. At other times, programmers may be interested in trying out techniques that are entirely new to them. In all such cases, an experienced, capable programmer should be available to assist user personnel through a telephone call or a visit.

Reliability

The reliability of the timesharing utility itself is an important consideration for any prospective user. As most prospective users are well aware, the timesharing field has been littered with corporate corpses. If a timesharing company fails, the equipment manufacturer will typically repossess its equipment immediately. With the equipment, all too frequently, go the files developed at great expense and with much difficulty by user companies.

Thus the startup phase of any program for initiating timesharing services should include a businessman's evaluation of the stability and likely continuity of operation of the timesharing company itself. This point should need no further elaboration. A timesharing supplier should be considered in much the same light as a vendor of heavy equipment. A company buying a piece of production machinery would want to satisfy itself as to the continuing availability of parts and service. When a company begins using timesharing, it should go to similar lengths to satisfy itself that the vendor will continue to exist and function reliably.

Consideration of the reliability of a timesharing utility may include consideration of the performance of one or more of its own vendors. For example, computer downtime—the periods when a computer is out of service for either scheduled or unscheduled maintenance—can affect the ability of users to access and derive results from a system. Thus, if a timesharing utility uses a particular make or model of computer that has proved unreliable, this could affect a prospective user's decision.

Similarly, if the timesharing utility is in an area that has experienced interference or unreliable service with communication lines, this should also be considered. Some areas of the country are more subject than others to what is called "line noise"— electrical interference that garbles data communication signals. Similarly, some types of telephone central office equipment are more subject than others to noise or service interruption. As indicated earlier, the reliability of communication services can be determined best by talking to other users. The same, in general, is true about a determination of whether a timesharing service suffers unreasonably high amounts of "downtime." Obviously, any user considering continuing application of timesharing techniques should analyze the reliability and projected continuity of service for each vendor being considered.

Suppliers' Commitments and Interests

The commitments and interests of the managements of timesharing utilities being considered as suppliers are also important decision factors. These considerations should be reviewed with a concern for the operating continuity of the individual timesharing system under development. Questions that might be asked include these:

- Do the services being proposed represent a major effort and commitment on the part of the timesharing utility or is this simply a sideline?
- What can be learned about the timesharing utility? Does it look as though its management will continue to support the services under consideration or is the company likely to head off in other directions?
- Do the services offered by the timesharing company have a broad enough market base to assure the continuation of the business and of the specific services being considered?
- Is the company keeping up with its competitors in the service area under consideration?

ESTIMATING COSTS

The costs of timesharing services are not always so apparent or so easy to predict as the uninitiated prospective user might expect. Fee structures are likely to present a particular challenge for users contemplating problem-solving applications, because the charges for such systems are frequently calculated through complex formulas that require application of the timesharing computer itself.

Elements of Cost

Charges for timesharing services can be hard to analyze, once they have been levied. A number of different factors may be involved in their computation. One common factor, for example, is a charge per hour, or per minute, for the time that the user's terminal is actually connected to the system. Another charge factor may be the amount of central processor time actually expended on user programs. Some timesharing services are billing on the basis of what are known as "computer resource units" (CRUs)—a factor developed on a weighted basis to include the file capacity, computer time, and support equipment needed to handle the user's job. In addition, some timesharing services levy monthly charges for file storage space utilized. Any given time-sharing utility may base its billing on one, some, or all of these factors. In some instances, the only way to estimate costs realistically is to actually run a benchmark job and have the timesharing utility render a bill.

Companies contemplating record-keeping applications may find themselves with entirely different sets of alternatives. Record-keeping applications are sometimes billed on the number of transactions, or line items, processed. In other cases, there may be a flat rate for the service, with incremental charges based on greater-than-minimum volumes.

The cost of terminals and associated communication equipment and lines can also be a significant factor in the operating costs of a timesharing system. As discussed in Chapter 2, there are many different varieties of terminals, communication devices, and line capabilities—each representing different tradeoffs between costs and capabilities. In evaluating the costs of a timesharing system, therefore, terminal and communication equipment must be considered thoroughly.

Terminals: Rent or Buy?

Evaluation of terminal and communication equipment costs should include consideration of whether it is economically advantageous to rent or buy such equipment. Also, consideration should be given to the cost of operating the terminal once it has been installed. The responsible manager should estimate data entry volumes and determine whether full-time or part-time personnel are required to handle these functions. Costs should be estimated both for the training of personnel and for the continuing services they will provide to the ongoing application.

As a general rule, the new timesharing user is well advised to rent, rather than buy, terminals. Innovations in and new designs for on-line terminals are among the fastest-growing areas of data-processing equipment development. Accordingly, the obsolescence of existing equipment also occurs at an extremely fast rate.

There may be exceptions, of course; a company's application itself may be static in nature. The individual manager is in the best position to evaluate the cost and other implications of rent-or-buy decisions.

A word of caution is, however, in order. Large numbers of timesharing terminals have been sold by salesmen who present lease-purchase options that cost very little more—perhaps $20 or $30 per month—then the conventional rental price. At the end of two or three years, the user owns the terminal. However, this may prove to be a dubious distinction. At the end of two or three years, the user may find himself in possession of obsolete equipment. In many cases, the user would have been better off to rent the equipment at the lower price and maintain the flexibility to change when something better came on the market.

How to Pinpoint Costs

No matter what the application, the prospective user should make a specific effort to pinpoint costs before going ahead with the major commitment that most timesharing ventures represent. If the user is contemplating a record-keeping application using standardized programs, it is possible to estimate the timesharing utility's charges in advance with a high degree of accuracy. The user simply specifies the volumes of work he anticipates, then asks the utility to provide a statement of what it would cost to process this amount of work.

For the company contemplating problem-solving applications, advance cost estimates are more difficult to obtain. The situation here is that it is impossible to pinpoint costs exactly until jobs are actually run. Even if a user has samples of what his finished reports should look like and sets of actual input data, it may still be impossible to estimate costs with any precision until programs have actually been run on the facilities of the particular timesharing utility under consideration. Bear in mind that there may be wide variations in costs for processing the same job on different computers—variations resulting from factors discussed earlier, such as the configuration and size of the computer and software support.

For the company contemplating a problem-solving application of substantial proportions, it will probably be worthwhile to develop and run a relatively complete benchmark problem. As described earlier, this benchmark problem would represent a small portion of the full program to be developed. It would actually be programmed, however, so that data could be entered and processed, and end results delivered. Running this benchmark problem on alternative timesharing utilities' computers can help greatly in developing cost estimates for the full program.

In any case, it is important that the responsible manager develop reliable estimates of costs at an early point in the timesharing project. Decisions based on these costs can then follow conventional management logic. If the timesharing project will replace an existing system within the company, cost comparisons can be made directly. If the project is aimed at developing a capability that does not currently exist within the company, then some effort should be made to ascribe a value to the anticipated results.

Frequently Overlooked Costs

Costs frequently overlooked by managers evaluating the potential of timesharing systems include the expenses of developing the system itself. One reason that this expense item is sometimes not given adequate consideration is that the services involved are frequently not provided by the timesharing utility. Typically, a timesharing utility representative will provide minimum-cost data as guidelines for the prospective user. Typically also, the timesharing utility representative will indicate that the user company can develop its own systems and procedures. Unfortunately, this is frequently not the case. In timesharing as elsewhere in data processing, system design is the area in which cost overruns are experienced most consistently. Therefore, the project aimed at developing and implementing a timesharing system should pay particular attention to system design and development costs.

There are, in particular, two primary development costs that should be evaluated in the course of establishing a timesharing system: the coding of programs and the input of data to establish processing files. The actual design and writing of programs will be a major factor—in many cases *the* major factor—for companies initiating problem-solving applications on timeshared computers. The extent of the programming effort, obviously, will depend on whether the timesharing utilities being considered have existing packages that can be used. If so, a determination should also be made of the extent to which such packages may have to be modified or supplemented by additional programming.

The approach to and cost of programming will depend on the situation of the individual company. If the company has an existing data-processing capability, a decision may be made to have the programming staff handle this work. If so, the programming manager should be asked to project and estimate the costs of the timesharing programming effort. To the extent possible, responsibility should be established for the accuracy and reliability of these estimates. As anyone who has been involved in system development knows, estimates of programming costs can vary widely in reliability and accuracy. This point will not be belabored here. However, if the company is already doing programming, estimates should be prepared under the best available techniques.

The obvious alternative is to have programming done by an outside vendor—possibly the timesharing utility itself. If this course is to be followed, the responsible manager should be sure that end results to be delivered by the contractor's programs are defined in advance and that fees are preestablished.

As a further consideration, a company that contracts for outside programming services should either have or plan to establish an in-house capability to maintain programs once they are operational. In most cases, it will not be feasible to subcontract small modifications of existing programs. It is far more desirable to have someone on the company's own staff trained to handle program maintenance. This training can frequently be implemented through the capabilities of a timesharing service. However, the costs of such training and maintenance of capabilities by the staff personnel involved should be taken into consideration.

The setting up of files to support the timesharing system will, in most cases, represent a greater expense for the user with a record-keeping application than for the user with a problem-solving application. This is simply because the files that support record-keeping applications are far more extensive.

Consideration should be given to the method that will be used to set up application files at the timesharing utility. In some cases, this can be done by the company's own personnel, with input handled on-line from the operating terminal. In other cases, the file conversion effort can be subcontracted to an outside service bureau. In such cases, it may be more desirable to set up the initial files on punched cards, on magnetic tape, or possibly on magnetic disks.

Whichever file conversion procedure is followed, care should be taken to ensure that accuracy and balance are established before actual application processing begins. This factor should be considered for its impact on reliability as well as on costs.

Cost Impact of the Processing Approach

The processing approach used in a particular timesharing application can have a major impact on both cost and efficiency. Specifically, users may wish to consider the alternatives between interactive entry and processing of transactions and remote batch entry and processing at lower-cost times of the computer's operating day.

In most cases, the alternative of remote batch processing will apply primarily to record-keeping applications. In problem-solving situations, transaction volumes will tend to be comparatively lower than for record-keeping applications, and so will the potential savings through remote batch processing. In addition, as discussed in Chapter 8, the rapid turnaround available through interactive processing is more important in problem-solving applications that call for direct interaction by top management.

In many record-keeping situations, however, it may be entirely feasible to capture transactions on storage media—such as punched tapes or magnetic cassettes—created at the terminal throughout the business day. Typically, these transaction records are transmitted to the timesharing utilities during low-volume, low-cost evening hours. Transmissions are in batches, frequently with their own control totals for processing verification. Rather than using terminal and communication line time for printing under such circumstances, the required output documents and reports are created on high-speed printers at the computer center and delivered by messengers.

The use of remote batch techniques promises to expand in the foreseeable future, particularly with the continuing introduction of so-called "intelligent" terminals. These units, as discussed in Chapter 2, have their own electronic capacities for validating transaction formats, account numbers, and other data elements within transactions. Such terminals are, increasingly, being made available with magnetic-tape cassettes that can store transactions for high-speed batch transmission to timesharing computers. Such terminals are being provided in both general-purpose and special-industry configurations.

As part of almost any developmental effort that will result in a record-keeping application on a timesharing computer, the responsible manager should probably consider and compare the cost-effectiveness of interactive and remote batch processing alternatives.

Some Typical Examples

Some typical examples of cost elements that will be encountered in the development of timesharing systems are as follows:

- The cost of connecting a terminal to the timesharing system can vary widely, from $2.50 to $20 per hour. In some cases, record-keeping applications charge a flat monthly fee— ranging up to $1000—for establishing a dedicated portal for the user's terminal to interact with the system.
- Terminal rental costs can range from $50 to $300 per month. Terminal purchases can range from $1000 to $7000.

- Processing time costs—as a general, extremely rough, rule of thumb—will be about the same per minute as the charge per hour for terminal connect time. Thus the range can be anywhere from $2.50 to $20 per processing minute.
- File storage costs are generally based on a flat fee per month for each 1000 characters maintained in the files. These charges can vary widely—from 15 cents up to $2 per 1000 characters.

CONSIDERING THE ALTERNATIVES

Alternative techniques for processing the same job or jobs on equipment other than timesharing computers should also be considered. Such consideration can have a bearing both on the cost-effectiveness and on the operating efficiency of the finished system.

Obviously, consideration of techniques other than timesharing is beyond the scope of this volume. However, the responsible manager should be aware that the types of job that lend themselves well to timesharing processing can also be excellent candidates for other low-cost data-processing methods, including:

- Punched-card accounting machines.
- Electronic bookkeeping machines.
- Minicomputers.
- Programmable electronic calculators.

In general, the same development cycle described here for the initiation of a timesharing system is also needed to handle the same applications with other, stand-alone techniques and equipment. Therefore, the logical place to consider such alternatives is during the cost estimating phase of a timesharing development project.

SYSTEM DESIGN AND DEVELOPMENT

System design and development activities should follow the initial feasibility evaluations of timesharing utility capabilities and costs. System design and development, as any experienced manager knows, are the highest-cost elements of any effort that brings a company into operational use of a data-processing system.

For the purposes of this discussion, it will be assumed that the manager responsible for a timesharing system development project either possesses or has access to experience or expertise in some phase of systems development. Specifically, there are areas of similarity between the development of a timesharing system or a batch computer processing system. These similarities exist in the basic structure of a project. The effort begins with a defining of objectives and results. Inputs and data files must then be defined. In general, the project must be set up in a series of planned steps, with interspersed checkpoints. All of these approaches are equally appropriate to the development of a timesharing system.

Within a timesharing system, however, there are certain unique considerations for which special provisions should be made. These a timesharing system.

- System design efforts should concentrate on making effective use of the computer terminal and its interactive capabilities. For example, procedures can be set up under which instructions are printed at the terminal that, in effect, guide the operator through each transaction to be entered. Diagnostic or instructional messages can be sent to the operator when erroneous entries are made. Also, transaction data can be validated as they are entered. In processing the entry of a part number, for example, the computer can verify that the part number actually exists on the user's files before accepting the input. Effective terminal procedures contribute significantly to the advantages of accuracy, reliability, and productivity made available through timesharing systems.

- Specific provision should be made for procedures to be followed when a user experiences an interruption in the services provided by a timesharing utility. *For problem-solving applications,* the routine procedure may simply be to wait a little while and try again. However, if interruptions continue, the company may consider either changing services or setting up programs that make it possible to use two or more services alternatively. *For record-keeping applications,* the establishment of alternate, off-line procedures is mandatory.

Management should be sure that reports produced regularly by the timesharing service provide a basis for such alternate procedures. When service continues for a long period without interruption, many managers have found it valuable to stage the equivalent of fire drills—purposeful interruptions of service for short periods to test the backup procedures.

* Special attention should be paid to the areas of data control, audit trail documentation, and the confidentiality of files maintained within timesharing computer systems. With a timesharing system, a special dimension of delegation of responsibility for information custody is present. This matter was discussed in Chapter 3. However, in considering the design of a new system, the responsible manager should be sure that provisions have been made that will satisfy his company's management—and its auditors.

* If programming is to be done on an interactive basis, special attention should be paid to the initial planning and documentation of a timesharing effort. To be handled effectively, programming should be a disciplined process. With the use of a timesharing terminal, much of the discipline of conventional coding sheets can be lost. In particular, a programmer who tests small modules of coding on a timesharing system may be tempted to patch a few individual instructions here and there to see if he can get the program module to run. When the results are satisfactory, the temptation is to go ahead with the next job. Such practices erode the discipline of documentation and lead to problems later on, when undocumented programs need revision.

IN SUMMARY

It cannot be too strongly emphasized that both management attention and a well-managed development effort are essential if a company is to realize its full potential benefit from the use of a timesharing system. Projects to develop timesharing systems for a user organization should be conducted on an orderly, controlled, responsibility-oriented basis.

With such a foundation, getting started in timesharing should be an exciting and rewarding experience.

Appendix A Directory of Timesharing Suppliers

The following directory of timesharing suppliers consists of two parts:

1. A listing of 98 timesharing suppliers in the United States and Canada, including their addresses and telephones.
2. A chart indicating the application programs available from each of these suppliers.

All of the material in this appendix has been extracted, with permission, from a DATAPRO 70 report, *All About Remote Computing Services.* (Copyright © 1975 by Datapro Research Corporation.) The complete report is available for $10 from the publishers, Datapro Research Corporation, 1805 Underwood Boulevard, Delran, New Jersey 08075.

The 98 timesharing suppliers included in this directory represent those that responded, out of some 200 companies known or believed to be in the remote computing business, to repeated requests for information from the Datapro Research survey staff. The absence of any specific company from this directory means that the company either failed to respond to the survey requests or was unknown to the Datapro Research staff.

The information included in this directory is the most recent available from Datapro Research Corporation as of February 1975. More current information will be available in subsequent editions of the annual DATAPRO 70 report.

152

ADDRESSES OF SUPPLIERS

ACTS Computing Corporation, 29200 Southfield Road, Southfield, Michigan 48076. Telephone (313) 557-6800.

APL Services, Inc., 684 Whitehead Road, Trenton, New Jersey 08638. Telephone (609) 883-0050.

Applied Computer Timesharing, Box 10188, Denver, Colorado 80210. Telephone (303) 771-0476.

Applied Data Processing, Inc., 33 Bernhard Road, North Haven, Connecticut 06473. Telephone (203) 787-4107.

Applied Data Research, Inc., Timesharing Division, Route 206 Center, Princeton, New Jersey 08540. Telephone (609) 921-8550.

Applied Logic Corporation, 900 State Road, Princeton, New Jersey 08540. Telephone (609) 924-7800.

Aquila BST (1974) Ltee/Ltd., C.P. 10 Tour de la Bourse, Montreal, Quebec 114Z 1A4.

Axicom Systems, Inc., 615 Winters Avenue, Paramus, New Jersey 07652. Telephone (201) 262-8200.

Beloit Computer Center, Inc., 423 State Street, Beloit, Wisconsin 53511. Telephone (608) 365-2206.

Boeing Computer Services, Inc., Eastern District, 7598 Colshire Drive, McLean, Virginia 22101. Telephone (703) 356-6900.

Bowne Time Sharing, Inc., 345 Hudson Street, New York, New York 10014. Telephone (212) 741-4700.

Chi Corporation, 11000 Cedar Avenue, Cleveland, Ohio 44106. Telephone (216) 229-6400.

Community Computer Corporation, 185 West Schoolhouse Lane, Philadelphia, Pennsylvania 19144. Telephone (215) 849-1200.

Computel Systems Limited, 1200 St. Lawrence Boulevard, Ottawa, Ontario K1K 3B8. Telephone (613) 746-4353.

The Computer Company, Inc., Seventh and Franklin Building, Richmond, Virginia 23219. Telephone (804) 644-1841.

Computer Innovations, 70 West Hubbard Street, Chicago, Illinois 60610. Telephone (312) 329-1561.

Computer Network Corporation (Comnet), 5185 MacArthur Boulevard, Washington, D.C. 20016. Telephone (202) 244-1900.

Computer Research Company, 200 North Michigan Avenue, Chicago, Illinois 60601. Telephone (312) 346-1331.

Computer Resource Services, Inc., 1600 West Camelback Road, Suite 1F, Phoenix, Arizona 85015. Telephone (602) 266-8444.

Computer Sciences Canada, Ltd., Room 367, Place du Canada, Montreal 101, Quebec. Telephone (514) 878-9811.

Computer Sciences Corporation, 650 North Sepulveda, El Segundo, California 90245. Telephone (213) 678-0311.

Computer Sharing Services, Inc., 2498 West Second Avenue, Denver, Colorado 80223. Telephone (303) 934-2381.

Computer Spectrum, Box 8666, Chattanooga, Tennessee 37411. Telephone (615) 396-3131.

Computility Division, Grumman Data Systems Corporation, 31 Tremont Street, Boston, Massachusetts 02111. Telephone (617) 423-6780.

Computone Systems, Inc., 361 East Paces Ferry Road N.E., Atlanta, Georgia 30305. Telephone (404) 261-0070.

Com-Share, Incorporated, P.O. Box 1588, Ann Arbor, Michigan 48106. Telephone (313) 994-4800.

Com-Share Limited, 41 Voyager Court North, Rexdale, Ontario. Telephone (416) 678-1363.

Control Data Corporation, Cybernet Services, P.O. Box 0, Minneapolis, Minnesota 55440. Telephone (612) 853-8100.

Cyphernetics Corporation, 175 Jackson Plaza, Ann Arbor, Michigan 48106. Telephone (313) 769-6800.

Data Resources Inc., 29 Hartwell Avenue, Lexington, Massachusetts 02173. Telephone (617) 369-7853.

Data-Tek Corporation, University City Science Center, 3401 Market Street, Philadelphia, Pennsylvania 19104. Telephone (215) 349-9900.

Datacrown Limited, 650 McNicoll Avenue, Willowdale, Ontario. Telephone (416) 499-1012.

Dataline Systems Limited, 40 St. Clair Avenue West, Toronto, Ontario. Telephone (416) 964-9515.

Datalogics, Inc., 11001 Cedar Avenue, Cleveland, Ohio 44106. Telephone (216) 721-9035.

Dialcom, Inc., 1104 Spring Street, Silver Spring, Maryland 20910. Telephone (301) 588-1572.

Fedder Data Centers, Inc., 412 West Redwood Street, Baltimore, Maryland 21201. Telephone (301) 685-6773.

First Data Corporation, 400 Totten Pond Road, Waltham, Masschusetts 02154. Telephone (617) 890-6701.

Fulton National Bank, 55 Marietta Street, Atlanta, Georgia 30302. Telephone (404) 577-3500.

General Electric Company, Information Services Business Division, 7735 Old Georgetown Road, Bethesda, Maryland 20014. Telephone (301) 654-9360.

Genesee Computer Center, Inc., 20 University Avenue, Rochester, New York 14605. Telephone (716) 232-7050.

Grumman Data Systems Corporation, 20 Crossways Park North, Woodbury, New York 11797. Telephone (516) 575-3284.

GTE Data Services Incorporated, First Financial Tower, P.O. Box 1548, Tampa, Florida 33601. Telephone (813) 224-3131.

HDR Systems, Inc., 8404 Indian Hills Drive, Omaha, Nebraska 68114. Telephone (401) 393-5775.

Honeywell Information Systems, Inc., 2701 Fourth Avenue South, Minneapolis, Minnesota 55408. Telephone (612) 332-5200.

Information Systems Design, Inc., 3205 Coronado Drive, Santa Clara, California 95051. Telephone (408) 249-8100.

Interactive Data Corporation, 486 Totten Pond Road, Waltham, Massachusetts 02154. Telephone (617) 890-1234.

Interactive Sciences Corporation, 60 Brooks Drive, Braintree, Massachusetts 02184. Telephone (617) 848-2660.

International Timesharing Corporation, I T S Building, Jonathon Industrex, Chaska, Minnesota 55318. Telephone (612) 448-3061.

Kaman Aerospace Corporation, Old Windsor Road, Bloomfield, Connecticut 06002. Telephone (203) 242-4461.

Keydata Canada, 74 Victoria Street, Toronto, Ontario. Telephone (416) 362-7681.

Keydata Corporation, 108 Water Street, Watertown, Massachusetts 02172. Telephone (617) 924-1200.

Leasco Response Incorporated, 20030 Century Boulevard, Germantown, Maryland 20767. Telephone (301) 428-0500.

Management Systems Corporation, 125 North State Street, Salt Lake City, Utah 84103. Telephone (801) 531-1122.

Manufacturing Data Systems, Inc., 320 North Main Street, Ann Arbor, Michigan 48104. Telephone (313) 761-7750.

Mark/Ops, Division of Northeastern Systems Associates, Inc., 475 Commonwealth Avenue, Boston, Massachusetts 02215. Telephone (617) 266-1930.

McDonnell Douglas Automation Company, P.O. Box 516, St. Louis, Missouri 63166. Telephone (314) 232-4640.

Metridata Computing, Inc., P.O. Box 21099, Louisville, Kentucky 40221. Telephone (502) 361-7161.

Multiple Access Limited, 885 Don Mills Road, Don Mills, Ontario. Telephone (416) 443-3900.

National CSS, Inc., 300 Westport Avenue, Norwalk, Connecticut 06581. Telephone (203) 853-7200.

Newfoundland and Labrador Computer Service, P.O. Box 9308, St. John's, Newfoundland.

Ohio Valley Data Control, Inc., 2505 Washington Boulevard, Belpre, Ohio 45714. Telephone (614) 423-9501.

On-Line Business Systems, Inc. One Embarcadero Center, San Francisco, California 94111. Telephone (415) 576-4222.

On-Line Systems Inc., 115 Evergreen Heights Drive, Pittsburgh, Pennsylvania 15229. Telephone (412) 931-7600.

Pacific Applied Systems, Inc., 4835 Van Nuys Boulevard, Suite 108, Sherman Oaks, California 91403. Telephone (213) 986-7515.

Pacific International Computing Corporation, 50 Beale Street, San Francisco, California 94105. Telephone (415) 764-9990.

Paden Data Systems, Inc., 5838 Live Oak, Dallas, Texas 75214. Telephone (214) 823-3773.

Philco-Ford Corporation, Computer Services Network, 515 Pennsylvania Avenue, Fort Washington, Pennsylvania 19304. Telephone (215) CH 8-2334.

Phoenix Data Limited, 550 Berry Street, Winnipeg, Manitoba R3H OR9. Telephone (204) 786-5831.

Polycom Systems Limited, 133 Wynford Drive, Don Mills, Ontario. Telephone (416) 449-3400.

PRC Computer Center, Inc., 7670 Old Springhouse Road, McLean, Virginia 22101. Telephone (703) 893-4880.

Programs & Analysis, Inc., 21 Ray Avenue, Burlington, Massachusetts 01803. Telephone (617) 272-7723.

Proprietary Computer Systems, Inc., 16625 Saticoy Street, Van Nuys, California 91406. Telephone (213) 781-8221.

Pryor Corporation, 400 North Michigan Avenue, Chicago, Illinois 60611. Telephone (312) 644-5650.

Rapidata, Inc., 20 New Dutch Lane, Fairfield, New Jersey 07006. Telephone (201) 227-0035.

Remote Computing Corporation, 1076 East Meadow Circle, Palo Alto, California 94303. Telephone (415) 328-5230.

Scientific Process & Research, Inc., 24 North Third Avenue, Highland Park, New Jersey 08904. Telephone (201) 846-3477.

Scientific Time Sharing Corporation, 7316 Wisconsin Avenue, Bethesda, Maryland 20014. Telephone (301) 657-8220.

Sci-Tek Incorporated, 1707 Gilpin Avenue, Wilmington, Delaware 19800. Telephone (302) 658-2431.

The Service Bureau Company, 500 West Putnam Avenue, Greenwich, Connecticut 06830. Telephone (203) 661-0001.

I.P. Sharp Associates Limited, Suite 1400, 145 King Street West, Toronto, Ontario. Telephone (416) 364-5361.

The Singer Company, Information Systems Network, 150 Totowa Road, Wayne, New Jersey 07470. Telephone (201) 256-5004.

Standard Information Systems, Inc. 36 Washington Street, Wellesley Hills, Massachusetts 02181. Telephone (617) 237-2910.

Statistical Tabulating Corporation, 2 North Riverside Plaza, Chicago, Illinois 60606. Telephone (312) 346-7300.

Structural Dynamics Research Corporation, 5729 Dragon Way, Cincinnati, Ohio 45227. Telephone (513) 272-1100.

Systems Dimensions Limited, 770 Brookfield Road, Ottawa, Ontario K1V 6J5. Telephone (613) 731-6910.

Technical Advisors, Inc., 4455 Fletcher Street, Wayne, Michigan 48184. Telephone (313) 722-5010.

Technology for Information Management, Inc., 1654 Central Avenue, Albany, New York 12205. Telephone (518) 869-0928.

Tel-A-Data, Inc., 1500 Northwest 167th Street, Miami, Florida 33169. Telephone (305) 625-8266.

Telstat Systems, Inc., 150 East 58th Street, New York, New York 10022. Telephone (212) 826-0640.

Time Sharing Resources, Inc., 777 Northern Boulevard, Great Neck, New York 11022. Telephone (516) 487-0101.

Tymshare, Inc., 10340 Bubb Road, Cupertino, California 95014. Telephone (408) 257-6550.

Uni-Coll, 3401 Science Center, Philadelphia, Pennsylvania 19104. Telephone (215) EV 7-3890.

United Computing Systems, Inc., 2525 Washington, Kansas City, Missouri 64108. Telephone (816) 221-9700.

University Computing Company, 7720 Stemmons Freeway, P.O. Box 47911, Dallas, Texas 75247. Telephone (214) 637-5010.

USS Engineers and Consultants, Inc., 600 Grant Street, Pittsburgh, Pennsylvania 15230. Telephone (412) 433-6515.

Wang Computer Services, Division of Wang Laboratories, Inc., 836 North Street, Tewksbury, Massachusetts 01876. Telephone (617) 837-4111.

Westinghouse Tele-Computer Systems Corporation, 2040 Ardmore Boulevard, Pittsburgh, Pennsylvania 15221. Telephone (412) 256-7799.

Xerox Computer Services, 5310 Beethoven Street, Los Angeles, California 90066. Telephone (213) 390-3461.

AVAILABILITY OF APPLICATION PROGRAMS*

COMPANY \ APPLICATION	Accounts payable	Accounts receivable	Banking	Billing	Data base management	Educational	Engineering	General ledger	Hospital administration	Information retrieval	Insurance	Inventory control	Numerical control	Operations research	Payroll	Personnel	Project control	Sales analysis	Scheduling	School administration	Scientific	Simulation	Statistical	Text editing	Typesetting
ACTS Computing Corporation	●	●			●	●	●	●	●	●		●	●	●	●	●	●	●	●	●	●	●	●	●	
APL Services, Inc.	●	●		●	●		●	●		●		●		●	●	●	●	●	●		●	●	●	●	
Applied Computer Timesharing	●	●	●	●						●					●				●						
Applied Data Processing, Inc.							●								●	●		●			●	●	●	●	
Applied Data Research, Inc.										●											●	●	●	●	
Applied Logic Corporation	●	●	●	●	●	●				●	●				●						●	●	●	●	●
Aquila BST	●	●	●	●	●		●	●		●								●	●		●	●	●		
Axicom Systems, Inc.					●					●		●			●		●								
Beloit Computer Center, Inc.					●																				
Boeing Computer Services, Inc.	●	●	●	●	●	●	●	●		●	●	●	●	●	●	●	●	●	●	●	●	●	●	●	●
Bowne Time Sharing, Inc.							●			●							●				●	●	●	●	●
Chi Corporation					●		●			●		●		●	●	●	●	●	●	●	●	●	●	●	●
Community Computer Corporation	●	●	●	●	●		●	●		●		●			●		●	●	●		●	●	●	●	
Computel Systems Limited	●	●		●	●	●	●			●	●	●	●	●	●		●	●	●		●	●	●	●	
The Computer Company, Inc.					●					●									●		●	●	●	●	
Computer Innovations	●	●	●		●	●	●	●	●	●	●	●		●	●	●	●	●	●		●	●	●	●	●
Computer Network Corporation	●	●	●	●	●					●		●		●	●		●	●			●	●		●	
Computer Research Company					●					●		●						●			●	●	●	●	
Computer Resource Services, Inc.	●	●		●						●												●	●	●	
Computer Sciences Canada, Ltd.	●	●			●					●		●		●			●	●			●	●	●	●	

Computer Sciences Corporation
Computer Sharing Services, Inc.
Computer Spectrum
Computility Division, Grumman
Computone Systems, Inc.

Com-Share, Incorporated
Com-Share Limited
Control Data Corporation
Cyphernetics Corporation
Data Resources Inc.

Data-Tek Corporation
Datacrown Limited
Dataline Systems Limited
Datalogics, Inc.
Dialcom, Inc.

Fedder Data Centers, Inc.
First Data Corporation
Fulton National Bank
General Electric Company
Genesee Computer Center, Inc.

Grumman Data Systems
GTE Data Services Incorporated
HDR Systems, Inc.
Honeywell Information Systems, Inc.
Information Systems Design

Interactive Data Corporation
Interactive Sciences Corporation
International Timesharing Corporation
Kaman Aerospace Corporation
Keydata Canada

AVAILABILITY OF APPLICATION PROGRAMS (Cont'd)*

COMPANY / APPLICATION	Accounts payable	Accounts receivable	Banking	Billing	Data base management	Educational	Engineering	General ledger	Hospital administration	Information retrieval	Insurance	Inventory control	Numerical control	Operations research	Payroll	Personnel	Project control	Sales analysis	Scheduling	School administration	Scientific	Simulation	Statistical	Text editing	Typesetting
Keydata Corporation	•	•		•	•							•			•		•	•	•		•	•	•	•	•
Leasco Response Incorporated	•	•	•	•			•	•	•		•			•	•	•	•	•	•		•	•	•	•	
Management Systems Corporation	•	•		•	•		•	•	•		•			•	•	•	•	•	•	•	•	•	•		•
Manufacturing Data Systems, Inc.	•	•	•		•								•												
Mark/Ops			•				•	•				•		•	•	•	•	•	•		•	•	•	•	•
McDonnell Douglas Automation Co.	•	•		•	•	•	•	•	•	•	•	•	•	•	•	•	•	•	•	•	•	•	•		
Metridata Computing, Inc.		•												•	•			•			•	•	•		
Multiple Access Limited	•	•		•	•			•		•		•		•	•	•	•	•			•	•	•	•	
National CSS, Inc.		•	•							•		•		•							•	•	•		
Newfoundland and Labrador Computer Service	•	•												•	•										
Ohio Valley Data Control, Inc.	•	•	•	•						•					•		•				•	•	•	•	•
On-Line Business Systems, Inc.		•			•					•		•		•		•	•				•	•			
On-Line Systems Inc.			•	•			•			•		•													
Pacific Applied Systems, Inc.					•					•					•										
Pacific International Computing Corp.					•					•															
Paden Data Systems, Inc.	•	•	•	•			•	•	•	•		•			•	•	•	•			•	•	•	•	•
Philco-Ford Comp. Serv. Network		•	•	•		•	•	•	•	•		•			•	•					•	•	•	•	•
Phoenix Data Limited	•	•		•				•	•	•					•						•	•	•	•	•
Polycom Systems Limited	•	•		•	•		•	•	•	•		•		•	•	•	•	•	•	•	•	•	•	•	•
PRC Computer Center, Inc.						•				•				•	•	•					•	•	•	•	•

Programs & Analysis Inc.
Proprietary Computer Systems, Inc.
Pryor Corporation
Rapidata, Inc.
Remote Computing Corporation

Scientific Process & Research, Inc.
Scientific Time Sharing Corp.
Sci-Tek Incorporated
The Service Bureau Company
I.P. Sharp Associates Limited

The Singer Company
Standard Information Systems, Inc.
Statistical Tabulating Corporation
Structural Dynamics Research Corp.
Systems Dimensions Limited

Technical Advisors, Inc.
Technology for Information Management
Tel-A-Data, Inc.
Telstat Systems, Inc.
Time Sharing Resources, Inc.

Tymshare, Inc.
Uni-Coll
United Computing Systems, Inc.
University Computing Company
USS Engineers and Consultants, Inc.

Wang Computer Services
Westinghouse Tele-Computer Systems
Xerox Computer Services

Appendix B Further
Reading

This appendix is a brief, selected bibliography of other books, information services, and recent articles on the subject of time-sharing.

The articles cover a wide range of computer timesharing applications, and should be especially valuable to readers of this book who are seeking more detailed information about certain types of timesharing applications or applications in a certain industry.

BOOKS, SERVICES, MISCELLANEOUS

Auerbach Information, Inc., *Auerbach on Time Sharing* (Philadelphia: Auerbach Information, Inc., 1970).

Bueschel, Richard T., Andrew G. Stephenson, and Douglas C. Whitney, *Commercial Time-Sharing Services and Utilities* (New York: American Management Association, 1969).

Caley, John D., *Computers for Small Business: Service Bureaus of Time-Sharing* (Washington, D.C.: Small Business Administration, U.S. Government Printing Office, 1971).

DATAPRO 70, *All About Remote Computing Services* (Delran, N.J.: Datapro Research Corporation, 1973).

Gateley, Wilson Y., and Gary C. Bitter, *BASIC for Beginners* (New York: McGraw-Hill Book Company, 1970).

Gregory, Robert H., and Richard L. Van Hern, *Automatic Data Processing Systems* (Belmont: Wadsworth Publishing Co., Inc., 1963).

Heaney, Donald F., *Development of Information Systems: What Management Needs to Know* (New York: The Ronald Press Co., 1968).

Popell, Steven D., et al., *Computer Time-Sharing: Dynamic Information Handling For Business* (Englewood Cliffs, N.J.: Prentice-Hall, Inc., 1966).

Wilkes, M. V., *Time-Sharing Computer Systems* (New York: American Elseview Publishing Co., Inc., 1968).

Ziegler, James R., *Time-Sharing Data Processing Systems* (Englewood Cliffs, N.J.: Prentice-Hall, Inc., 1967).

ARTICLES

Allen, Brandt, "Time Sharing Takes Off," *Harvard Business Review,* March-April 1969, pp. 128–136.

Andrew, William F., "Advantages of a Shared Computer," *Hospitals,* November 16, 1971, pp. 59–62.

Bigelow, Robert P., "Some Legal Aspects of Commercial Remote Access Computer Services," *Datamation,* August 1969, pp. 48–52.

Brewer, A. J., "Practical Applications of a Time-Sharing Computer Service in the State Income Tax Area," *TAXES: The Tax Magazine,* October 1971, pp. 620–626.

"Bright Spots in Time-Share Land (Remote Computing)," *Datamation,* January 15, 1971, p. 49.

Butler, Jay E., "TRIM: A Management Tool for Reviewing Inventory Practices," *The Arthur Young Journal,* Spring/Summer 1973, pp. 12–20.

Butler, Jay E., and D. W. Gibson, "Evaluation of Inventory Management," *Business Horizons,* June 1973, pp. 51–60.

Byrne, Edwin J., and Rudy A. Landry, "RAM-30: A Computer Model for Real Estate Investment Analysis," *The Arthur Young Journal,* Summer 1971, pp. 30–36.

"Cable TV Leaps Into the Big Time," *Business Week,* November 22, 1969, pp. 100–106+.

Coffey, Patricia, "Could Computer Create Triangle in a Marriage?," *Computer World,* May 28, 1969.

Colburn, Lynn, and James P. Magnell, "Time-Sharing Services," *Modern Data,* October 1968, pp. 34–36+.

Cushing, B. E., and Richard C. Rea, "Applications for Computer Time-sharing in Public Accounting," *Journal of Accountancy,* December 1970, pp. 76–79.

Donovan, Stephen F., "Time-Sharing Techniques," *Data Management,* September 1971, pp. 80–83.

Doran, Irwin, "Charlie Manoog and His Magnificent Accounting Machine," *Modern Office Procedures,* February 1969, pp. 27–31.

Dudgeon, Richard A., and Paul D. Fayollat, "Dynamic Environment Demands a Flexible Hospital Budget System," *Hospital Financial Management,* November 1973, pp. 30–37.

Dyment, John J., "Financial Planning with a Computer," *Financial Executive,* April 1970, pp. 34–44.

Ebeling, H. William, "Computer Time Sharing Systems," *Massachusetts CPA Review*, March-April 1971, pp. 20,22–23.

Eckstein, Otto, Edward Green, and V. Sundar Arajan, "New Approaches in Input-Output Analysis," *Business Economics*, January 1971, pp. 73–77.

Ellenberger, Frederick H., "Accountant and the Time-Share Terminal," *Management Accounting*, May 1971, pp. 39–40.

Fayollat, Paul D., "Computer Models: Two Ways To Do Financial Forecasts," *Modern Hospital*, April 1973, pp. 103–109.

Fayollat, Paul D., "HOSPLAN: A Financial Planning Model for Hospitals," *The Arthur Young Journal*, Winter 1972, pp. 17–25.

Friedman, J., "Minicomputer Timesharing: Filling the Cost Gap," *Data Dynamics*, July 1971, pp. 26–30.

Garoner, D., "Dartmouth's Time-Sharing System Captures College, Creates Confidence," *Datamation*, February 15, 1971, p. 47+.

"A Glimpse at the Future in Computer Centers: The Technical Computer Center at Ford Motor Company," *Computers and Automation*, January 1968, pp. 20–23.

Gross, D., "Actuarial Studies Assisted by Time-Sharing Computer Service," *Insurance*, Fall 1971, pp. 82+.

Guise, Robert F., Jr., "The '69 Time Sharing Gold Rush," *Datamation*, August 1969, pp. 38–42.

Haidinger, Timothy P., "Computer Timesharing: A New Tool for the Auditor," *Computer Auditing in the Seventies*, a special supplement to the Winter/Spring 1970 issue of *The Arthur Young Journal*, pp. 41–48.

Haidinger, Timothy P., "Computer Timesharing: A Primer for the Financial Executive," *Financial Executive*, February 1970, pp. 26–35.

Hirsch, P., "Multi-Access Computer Networks," *Datamation*, June 1970, pp. 153–4.

Hootman, Joseph T., "The Pricing Dilemma," *Datamation*, August 1969, pp. 61–66.

Howard, Phillip C., "Technology and Advantages of Time Sharing Systems," *Data Management*, August 1969, pp. 26–29.

Hutner, Alan H., "Taxes and Time Sharing," *TAXES: The Tax Magazine*, March 1971, pp. 140–68.

Ingram, Donald, "Time-Sharing Computer Terminal as a Modern Audit Tool," *GAO Review*, Winter 1971, pp. 71–76.

Karush, A. D., "Evaluating Time Sharing Systems Using the Benchmark Method," *Data Processing Magazine*, May 1970, pp. 42–44.

Katz, Alan D., "Ten Points to Consider in Selecting a Time-Sharing Computer Illustration Service," *CLU Journal*, July 1971, pp. 69-72.

Kaufman, Felix, "Computer Time Sharing for the CPA," *Management Services,* November-December 1968, pp. 17–29.

Main, Jeremy, "Computer Time-Sharing: Everyman at the Console," *Fortune,* August 1967, p. 88+.

Mastrogiovanni, Ronald D., and Daniel M. Morson, "Timesharing & the Auditor," *Modern Auditing: The Arthur Young Approach,* a special edition of the Autumn/Winter 1972-73 issue of *The Arthur Young Journal,* pp. 54–62.

Monczka, R. M., "Time-Shared Information Systems for Purchasing and Materials Management," *Journal of Purchasing,* May 1971, pp. 15–29.

"A New Industry's Wild Ride," *Business Week,* May 24, 1969, pp. 64–78.

Pancoast, J. W., Jr., "Time-Sharing for Word Processing," *Office,* February 1972, p. 60+.

Pantages, Angeline, "The Computer Utility: Implications for Higher Education," *Datamation,* August 1969, pp. 99–101.

"PERT, Critical Path Analysis Offered on Time Sharing Basis," *Management Adviser,* September 1971, p. 10.

Pointel, Nicole, and Daniel Cohen, "Computer Time Sharing: A Review," *Computers and Automation,* October 1967, pp. 38–46.

Robertson, J., "Time-Sharing Net to Widen at CDC," *Electronic News,* June 29, 1970, p. 1+.

Rosenberg, Arthur M., "The Brave New World of Time-Sharing Operating Systems," *Datamation,* August 1969, pp. 42–47.

Schultz, W. J., "Time-Sharing Provides Any Bank with Computer Assist," *Bankers Monthly,* August 1970, pp. 34–36.

Sloan, R. J., "Re-evaluating Time Sharing As a Business Tool," *Canadian Chartered Accountant,* July 1971, pp. 92–95.

Smith, Charles E., "Malfunction in Real-Time Systems," *Modern Data,* April 1969, pp. 62–64.

Smith, D. W., "Efficient Credit Management With Timesharing," *Financial Executive,* March 1971, pp. 26–30.

Sorensen, James L., "A Solution to the Small Company's EDP Dilemma," *Data Management,* April 1969, pp. 28–31.

Stewart, M., "Will Time-Sharing Help You?" *Management Review,* June 1970, pp. 37–41.

Szuprowicz, Bohdan O., "The Time-Sharing Users: Who Are They?" *Datamation,* August 1969, pp. 55–59.

Theis, D. J., and L. C. Hobbs, "Trends in Remote-Batch Terminals," *Datamation,* September 1, 1971, pp. 20–26.

"Time-Sharing Plan Gives Business Graphs from Computer Input," *Management Services*, January 1971, p. 14.

"Time-Sharing: What Is It?" *Auerbach Time Sharing Reports*, August 1969, pp. 1–30.

"Time-Sharing's New Breed of Entrepreneurs," *Modern Data*, April 1969, pp. 66–69.

Whitney, Douglas C., and Charles H. White, Jr., "Time-Sharing Services," *Modern Data Systems*, February 1968, pp. 40–50.

Wilkinson, Bryan, "A Six-Step Approach to Choosing a Time-Sharing Service," *Data Management*, December 1968, pp. 20–23.

Williams, Gwynn R., "Computer in Every Office," *Australian Accountant*, September 1971, pp. 341–342.

Woodfin, Paul B., "Time-Shared Computer Usage In the Corporate Tax Department," *Tax Executive*, April 1971, pp. 519–535.

Woronka, Theodore, "Program for Development," *Real Estate Today*, January 1972, pp. 42–45.

Index

Note: This index was prepared on a computer timesharing terminal.